# Prayer Works!

A STUDY GUIDE

# Kurt Johnson

HART RESEARCH CENTER
FALLBROOK, CALIFORNIA

Edited by Ken McFarland
Cover art direction and design by Ed Guthero
Cover illustration by Nathan Greene

The author assumes full responsibility for the
accuracy of all facts, quotations, and references as
cited in this book.

ISBN 1-878046-26-8

# Contents

Prayer Works!

# A Word From the Author

I am a different person today because of my efforts in preparing these study guides. The topics presented here have driven me to my knees and caused me to analyze my own prayer life. I have had to ask God for forgiveness where I have come short. And I have had to ask Him to make me a better man of prayer—a Spirit-filled man of prayer.

One cannot study God's biblical message to Christians about prayer and remain unchanged. It is my prayer for you and for myself that God will make us different people by the time we have completed these studies. May it be said of each of us, as God said of Saul, "The Spirit of the Lord will come upon you . . . and you will be turned into another man [person] . . . God gave him another heart." 1 Samuel 10:6, 9.

It is my prayer for you that each day, Jesus will become dearer to you as you grow in your communication with Him. May God be with you. Please pray for me—and I'll be praying for you.

Kurt Johnson

# Introduction

Many would consider the single most important principle in the life of a Christian to be what it has always been—to be a man or woman of prayer. For too long, Christianity has largely denied this principle. No matter who you are or what your status, a life not built on prayer will come to emptiness. Too many try to build their lives and ministries upon such foundations as hard work, education, materialism, sports, talent, or popularity. None of these work.

The fruits seen in our lives will be equal to the development of our inner walk with God. No matter how pure our motives, if there is no inner life, there will be no fruits of the Spirit.

Jesus did not tell Christians . . .

♦ to organize always

♦ to equip always

♦ to attend committees always

♦ to preach always.

But we *have* been told to *pray* always.

The greatest gift a Christian has to offer the world, the church, or his family is his or her personal life of prayer.

God shapes the world by prayer. The more people pray, the better life is. One may live in a society surrounded by the influence of sin, but the person who prays lives in an atmosphere that frustrates Satan. The praying Christian is protected by the strength and support of a victorious Saviour.

There is hope and faith in prayer. Prayer will make a radical difference in your life, in your identity as a person, and in your Christian experience.

# About Small Group
# Bible Study

Small Group Bible Study can be both enjoyable and educational. The small-group concept is not new — its foundations can be found in both the Old and New Testaments. The early church — in the time of Jesus and in the years that followed — was a community, home based Christian movement. Christian church buildings were virtually nonexistent in the Roman Empire until the time of Constantine.

Through the centuries, small groups have been called by such names as societies, classes, cottage meetings, and small companies. These study guides follow a format that has proven itself workable down through the years. The goal is for a group of interested people to meet in a home, public meeting room, church, or other location and study God's Word together. Ideally, the group will be three to twelve individuals sitting around a table or in a circle for an hour and a half to two hours, one day a week, studying, praying, and sharing together.

This experience should be relaxed and non-threatening. Often, group members come to the meeting from various religious backgrounds. Some may never have studied the Bible; this could be their first experience. Some may not know the location of Bible books, or how chapters and verses work together. Others will have studied for years; they can assist those just learning.

Prayer, Bible information, and opinions will be part of the group discussion. Some group members may never have prayed out loud before. Others will be quiet and shy. Still others will love to pray and talk. Be aware of these differences. Never use pressure or put anyone "on the spot." All discussion and prayer should be voluntary. As a general rule, do not go around the circle for prayer, answers, or discussion. Allow for spontaneous, voluntary responses. This makes the group more relaxed and enjoyable and allows for differences in personality and experience.

Three things are essential to all group Bible studies. Those essentials are 1) *sharing* (getting better acquainted with one another), 2) *Bible study* (understanding and learning about God's Word), and 3) *prayer* (applying what we have learned to personal life and asking God to assist us.)

The format suggested in this book is based on these three essentials and will be similar in each study. A brief description of each major section of the study guide lessons is as follows.

## Group Life

This section will provide an enjoyable beginning for each of your meetings. Some of the study guide lessons will discuss the dynamics of what can make your group life stimulating and enjoyable.

Also, your Bible study group should be a friendly experience. A non-threatening question to which group members may share their answers will assist them in becoming better acquainted with one another. This is a "fun" time that all will come to appreciate.

## Scripture and Life

Each lesson will also provide an introduction and background material that will shed light on the passages to be studied. As group members dialogue and compare one Scripture with another, the experience will result in a positive learning environment.

## Application to Life

We must keep in mind that Scripture is not only for study but also for living. Each group member will be given a private, personal moment to reflect on how he or she wishes to respond to the topic. The lesson then concludes with a reflection and prayer suggestion.

As you study the messages in each lesson, Scripture will be allowed to speak for itself, as God intended. Experience has shown that the topics of this series, when examined and applied to life, will assist group members in finding fulfillment and meaning in daily living. May God guide you as you open the fascinating pages of His message for our day.

# God Is Ready

"A great many people do not pray because they do not feel any sense of need. The sign that the Holy Spirit is in us is that we realize, not that we are full, but that we are emtpy." —Oswald Chambers.

## Group Life

One of the benefits of group Bible Study is the opportunity to develop close friendships with one another. As the weeks go by, your group members will become special to you. Prayer with God is similar. The more time we spend with God, the better we come to know Him.

Share with your group about what prayer was like in your home as a child. Did your family pray daily? At meals? Family worship? Who led out in prayer at your house: Dad? Mom? Grandma?

Note: If time permits, everyone in the group can share who wishes to share. If time is limited, only a few may have the opportunity. Remember that in group life, no one has to speak who does not want to share. Never just go around the circle. Instead, allow for a spontaneous response. This is a much more relaxed approach.

## Scripture and Life

The Scripture passage in our study is Luke 18:1-8. This parable of Jesus has been called by some the parable of the persistent widow. The setting is approximately March of A.D. 31. Lazarus has recently been raised from the dead, and it is a few weeks before the death of Jesus. Jesus has been discussing with His disciples some of the key ingredients in Christian living—forgiveness (17:1-4) and faith (17:5-10).

During a discussion with His disciples, the Jewish religious leaders interrupt Jesus. They ask Him when His kingdom will come. Jesus responds by telling His disciples about the events and signs of His coming. Directly following this instruction on end-time events, Jesus tells the parable of the persistent widow. Jesus connects this parable of prayer with living in the final days of earth's history.

## Luke 18:1-8 (NKJV)

1) Then He spoke a parable to them, that men always ought to pray and not lose heart, 2) saying: "There was in a certain city a judge who did not fear God nor regard man. 3) Now there was a widow in that city; and she came to him, saying, Avenge me of my adversary. 4) And he would not for a while; but afterward he said within himself, 'Though I do not fear God nor regard man, 5) yet because this widow troubles me I will avenge her, lest by her continual coming she weary me.' 6) Then the Lord said, "Hear what the unjust judge said. 7) And shall God not avenge His own elect who cry out day and night to Him, though He bears long with them? 8) I tell you that He will avenge them speedily. Nevertheless,

when the Son of Man comes, will He really find faith on the earth?"

## Verse 1:

❑ This is a parable (a story with a lesson) about prayer. What does it mean to pray always? Apply your definition and suggest an example of a daily prayer schedule.

_____

_____

❑ What does it mean to "not faint" (KJV) or "not to lose heart" (NKJV)?

_____

_____

_____

❑ Have you ever been discouraged because it appears that God isn't listening to your prayers?

_____

_____

❑ If you become discouraged about prayer, what do you do to overcome your discouragement?

_____

_____

Note: The Jewish leaders taught that people should pray three times a day (Daniel 6:10). Two of these times were during the time of the morning and evening sacrifices offered by the priests on Israel's behalf. The other time was at mid-day. Some rabbis taught that the people should not pray at other times, to avoid disturbing God. (See *SDA Bible Commentary*, vol. 5, p. 844.)

## Verse 2:

This verse introduces us to one of the main characters of the parable — the judge. This judge would probably have been a paid magistrate appointed by the Romans. Ordinary Jewish disputes were taken before the elders and not into the public courts. The Roman judges were notorious for their injustice. Unless a plaintiff had influence or money to bribe his way to a verdict, there was little hope for justice. The judges were often called by the people "robber judges." (See Barclay, *Luke*, pp. 221, 222.) Notice that Jesus does not specify a city or a specific person in this parable. He does not needlessly antagonize the people into charging Him with undermining the government.

❑ What does it mean that the judge did not fear God or regard man? What is another word for fear?

_____

_____

_____

❑ Describe how you think the judge would treat people today? Modernize the story.

_____

_____

_____

_____

## Verses 3-5:

This verse introduces the second character of the parable—the widow. Life is not easy when a spouse dies. However, being a widow today is usually much easier physically than it was in biblical times. A widow usually had no money, no property, no job, and no education. If she was fortunate enough to have a son or a relative to assist her, life was bearable. If the widow had no one, she could easily become a street person.

A beautiful characteristic of God is that He cares for all and watches out for their well being. A widow is no exception. James says it is "pure religion" to visit the widows "in their affliction" (James 1:27). Jesus spoke against the Pharisees because they "devour widow's houses" (Matthew 23:14).

This particular widow had an enemy—an adversary—who was causing her difficulty. It may be that the enemy was taking money or property from her. Whatever the case, there was no legal aid or court-appointed attorney available. The widow goes to the judge for assistance.

❑ What parallels do you observe between the widow's condition and the sinner?

_____

_____

_____

_____

_____

❑ At first, what was the judge's attitude toward the widow? (Verse 4)

_____

_____

❑ How did his attitude change? (Verses 4, 5)_____

_____

_____

❑ Why did he change his attitude?_____

_____

_____

Some, in studying this passage, stop at verse 5 and say, "I understand. I am to pray without ceasing to convince God of my need."

❑ Is the purpose of praying without ceasing to convince God of anything?

_____

❑ If not, why should we pray without ceasing?

_____

_____

## Verse 6-8:

This parable is a study in contrasts or opposites. Immediately after telling the story, Jesus interprets it.

❑ What is the contrast or point that Jesus wants the reader to understand?

_____

_____

_____

Suggestions:

♦ Compare the characters of the judge and God.

♦ Compare the judge's motives with God's motives.

♦ Compare the widow's condition and situation with that of a Christian or non-Christian. Are they similar?

♦ Compare the judge with God in their response to human needs.

♦ Discuss the judge's willingness to listen to the widow and God's willingness to listen to people on this earth.

❏ Who are the elect of verse 6?_____

_____

_____

❏ What does it mean to cry day and night?_____

_____

❏ How does God "bear long" with His people?

_____

_____

## Points to consider:

God may be "bearing long" — that is, appearing to delay His response, for the following reasons.

◆ God is putting into operation events that in the future will accomplish what is best for us.

◆ God may be allowing a negative situation to continue in order to give the persecutor time to repent.

◆ Delay may be to help develop our character.

◆ Delay intensifies our need of God.

Remember that 2 Peter 3:9 states: "God is not slack concerning His promise."

❏ What does Jesus mean when He asks: "Will he find faith at his coming?"_____

_____

❏ Why do you think Jesus concludes with this question?_____

_____

❏ From your study of this parable, what does it teach you about God's readiness for us to pray?

_____

_____

## A Final Thought . . .

The theme of this parable is that as Christians, we are not really like the widow. The widow was poor, powerless, and forgotten. The judge was a stranger to her. We are God's adopted sons and daughters. We are part of the family! The riches of heaven are available to us! The judge is nothing like our heavenly parent. God is righteous, loving, sympathetic, and just. We do not have to beg. God is standing with open arms to meet our needs.

He invites us to come to Him just as we are with our hurts, brokenness, and sin.

Look at His promises!

- ♦ "I am the way, the truth and the life" (John 14:6).

- ♦ "He shall deliver the needy when he cries; the poor also, and him that has no helper" (Psalm 72:12).

- ♦ "You will keep him in perfect peace whose mind is stayed on you, because he trusts in you" (Isaiah 26:3).

- ♦ "And all things, what ever you shall ask in prayer, believing, you will receive" (Matthew 21:22).

No voice in prayer is sweeter to God than yours. What are you waiting for? He is *ready!*

## Application to Life

At the conclusion of your group meeting, take time to pray together. Remember that not everyone is comfortable praying aloud in public. Some may never have been taught to pray. Because of this, never simply go around the circle, and never expect everyone to pray. As you pray, ask for special requests for prayer and for two volunteers to pray. Also, pray for your group members to grow in their prayer life. Begin your time by providing thirty seconds for silent prayer. At the conclusion, read the Lord's Prayer together:

*Our Father in heaven, hallowed be Your name. Your kingdom come. Your will be done on earth as it is in heaven. Give us this day our daily bread. And forgive us our debts, as we forgive our debtors. And do not lead us into temptation, but deliver us from the evil one. For Yours is the kingdom and the power and the glory forever. Amen.*

## LESSON 2

# What Is Prayer?

"Our asking and expecting and God's doing
jointly bring to pass things that otherwise would
not come to pass. Prayer changes things. This is
the great fact of prayer." —S.D. Gordon.

## Group Life

In the early 1970s, I had a discussion with a college
student in Manito Park in Spokane, Washington. The
student, whose name was Ken, did not believe in the
existence of God. As we discussed the topic together,
he asked me about the reason Christians pray. Ken
also wanted to know the Christian's definition of
prayer. This discussion caused me to focus on a part
of the Christian's relationship with God that is
sometimes taken for granted—prayer.

As this lesson begins, divide into sub-groups of
two or three, depending upon your group's size.
Each sub-group is to take five minutes and write a
definition of prayer in fifteen words or less. After five
minutes, each sub-group will share its definition with
the entire group. It is fine if the definitions are similar.

_____

_____

_____

_____

## Scripture and Life

Prayer is timeless. People may die, but the influence of their prayers goes on changing lives and the world. This is one reason it is important that Christians understand prayer.

Praying is not a natural instinct of life. Babies are not born praying. Children are not always taught reliance upon God. In fact, throughout the world society breathes the philosophy that self sufficiency is the foundation of life. But self sufficiency, which depends on one's "inner self," undermines the reason and need of prayer.

Numerous authors have defined prayer. And each attempts to include any phrase or characteristic he or she believes others may have omitted. But attempting to humanly define something of divine origin is very difficult—if not impossible. Nonetheless, in this study we will attempt to seek an answer to the question: What is prayer?

A biblical definition of prayer that we will discuss and study is that prayer is remaining (abiding) in God.

A Scripture passage that illustrates this definition is John 15:1-17 (NKJV).

1) I am the true vine, and My Father is the vinedresser. 2) Every branch in Me that does not bear fruit He takes away; and every branch that bears fruit He prunes, that it may bear more fruit. 3) You are already clean because of the word which I

have spoken to you. 4) Abide in Me, and I in you. As the branch cannot bear fruit of itself, unless it abides in the vine, neither can you, unless you abide in Me. 5) I am the vine, you are the branches. He who abides in Me, and I in Him, bears much fruit; for without Me you can do nothing. 6) If anyone does not abide in Me, he is cast out as a branch and is withered; and they gather them and throw them into the fire, and they are burned. 7) If you abide in Me, and My words abide in you, you will ask what you desire, and it shall be done for you. 8) By this My Father is glorified, that you bear much fruit; so you will be My disciples. 9) As the Father loved Me, I also have loved you; abide in My love. 10) If you keep My commandments, you will abide in My love, just as I have kept My Father's commandments and abide in His love. 11) These things I have spoken to you, that My joy may remain in you, and that your joy may be full. 12) This is My commandment, that you love one another as I have loved you. 13) Greater love has no one than this, than to lay down one's life for his friends. 14) You are My friends if you do whatever I command you. 15) No longer do I call you servants, for a servant does not know what his master is doing; out I have called you friends, for all things that I heard from My Father I have made known to you. 16) You did not choose Me, but I chose you and appointed you that you should go and bear fruit, and that your fruit should remain, that whatever you ask the Father in My name He may give you. 17) These things I command you, that you love one another.

The background of this passage is seen in the history and daily life of the Jewish nation. Numerous times in the Old Testament, Israel is pictured as the vine or (grape) vineyard of God (see Isaiah 5:1-7). "The vineyard of the Lord is the house of Israel." Hosea calls Israel a luxuriant vine (Hosea 10:1).

The vine, when Jesus spoke the words recorded in John 15, had actually become the symbol of the nation of Israel. A golden vine decorated the front of Herod's temple. Figures of the leaves of the vines and clusters of grapes were displayed on coins and architecture. Many considered it a great honor to give gold to those decorating the temple or other public edifices, to be used in molding a grape or a new bunch of grapes.

The grapevine was and still is grown all over Palestine. The plant needs a great deal of attention if the best fruit is to be produced. The ground needs to be kept free from weeds. The people sometimes train the vine to grow on trellises — or it sometimes creeps over the ground and is held up off the ground with forked sticks. The plant grows quickly, and drastic pruning is necessary to produce fruit and to keep the vine in order.

As Jesus observed the growth and care of the grapevine, He saw in it imagery that reflects the relationship between Himself and His people.

❑ Verses 1 and 2 introduce the main characters of the passage. Jesus identifies Himself as the vine and the Father as the one who takes care of the vineyard. Who is represented by the branches?

_____

❑ Who or what do you think is represented by the vineyard?

_____

_____

❑ Discuss the relationship of the grape plant's roots, vines, branches, and soil. Relate this to the application Jesus is making between the Father, Himself, and the Christian.

_____

_____

_____

To understand the answer to the question, "what is prayer?" as found in these verses of Scripture, one must first understand their primary theme. That theme is, "remaining in Jesus." To illustrate the theme, Jesus uses the analogy of the grapevine. He then introduces the theme of "remaining" by discussing fruit and pruning.

As we study this passage, let's study it as Jesus organized it. The sub-themes are fruit, pruning, and remaining.

## Fruit

The purpose of the grapevine is to produce grapes. Following this analogy or line of reasoning, what is the fruit the Christian is to produce?

To assist in your discussion, the following verses may be helpful. Galatians 5:22, 23; Ephesians 5:8-10; Philippians 1:9-11; Hebrews 12:11; James 3:13-18.

❑ What causes the fruit of the Christian life to grow in our daily lives?_____

_____

❑ What is the part of prayer in this process?_____

_____

_____

Now read 1 John 5:12, and then answer the following question:

❑ What kind of fruit would you like to see in your life?

   ❑ love for my neighbors and/or family

   ❑ patience

   ❑ ability to share my faith

   ❑ better prayer and Bible study habits

   ❑ compassion for the needy

   ❑ other_____

## Pruning

John 15:2 discusses two types of pruning. First, God cuts off every branch that bears no fruit, and then every branch that produces fruit is pruned so it will be more fruitful.

❑ What causes a branch (you) connected to the vine (Jesus) to not bear fruit?_____

_____

_____

❑ How is fruit-bearing related to a Christian's prayer life?_____

_____

_____

❑ In what ways does God prune the fruitful Christian's life?_____

_____

_____

❏ How does it feel to have your life pruned?

_____

_____

In Israel, pruning was a very important part of the gardener's or vineyard keeper's job. A young plant was drastically cut back for the first three years of its life to conserve its life and energy. When the plant became mature, it was pruned in December and January. If the branch that bore no fruit was not pruned, it would drain away the plant's strength. The unfruitful branches caused the remaining fruit to be less healthy and decreased the size of the cluster of grapes.

The fruitless, pruned branches were destroyed, because they were useless. The wood was too soft to be used for any purpose. For example, Jewish law stated that at various times during the year, the people were to bring wood for the altar fires. However, no wood from the grapevines was to be brought. It was considered to be useless and was burned in a bonfire.

As we study the message of producing fruit and pruning branches, obviously the first choice for most of us would be to become branches producing healthy fruit.

In order for this to occur, verses 4-8 state that we must remain in the vine, Jesus Christ.

## Remaining

❏ What does it mean in this passage when it says "to remain," or as other translations put it, "to abide" in Jesus?_____

_____

Verses 3 and 7 state that remaining involves the Word of God and talking with God ("ask"). This means that the ingredients of remaining are the same as the ingredients of a prayer life.

Christians communicate with God in various ways, but primarily by:

♦ reading the Bible

♦ talking to God about what they read in the Bible

♦ meditating on and memorizing the Scriptures that apply specifically to their need

♦ talking to God about their personal life and world

These four points arise out of verses 3 and 7. As one considers them, it is obvious that to sincerely spend time communicating with God involves a continual connection of the mind and heart with Him.

❏ Are you comfortable with the idea that prayer is a continual connection with God that occurs as we spend time with Him? (Yes or No.)_____

Read John 15:1-8 aloud. As you do, replace the words "remain" or "abide" with the phrase "spend time with."

After reading the verses this way, list some good reasons for having a regular appointment with God. One reason is given as an example. Add as many others as you observe in this passage.

☐ If you spend time with God, He will spend time with you (v. 4).

☐ _____

☐ _____

☐ _____

☐ _____

☐ _____

☐ _____

Recently a friend of mine named Fred told me that he was struggling in his relationship with Jesus. Fred said that since I had moved away from where he lived, he now had no friend to whom he could turn when he had problems in his Christian life. "When you were here," he said, "I could talk to you and spend time with you. I gained strength as we shared together."

Remaining in Jesus is something like what Fred shared with me. The secret of Jesus' life was His contact with His Father. The Bible says that Jesus withdrew from people numerous times to pray. We must take deliberate steps to maintain our contact with Jesus. This will mean arranging life, arranging prayer, and arranging time for silence so that we do not forget Him.

Verses 9-17 state that when we remain in Jesus, certain fruits or characteristics will be seen in our lives. List these fruits or characteristics:

◆ _____

◆ _____

◆ _____

◆ _____

◆ _____

In your personal life, what is true of your struggle to remain in the vine?

☐ busy schedule: no time for prayer

☐ tired: too much to do

☐ lonely: I feel like I am the only branch on the
    vine

☐ afraid: that I will be pruned off and discarded

☐ defeated: it is hard to remain in the vine

☐ other:_____

If you struggle in your prayer relationship with
Jesus, be encouraged! Two promises in verses 15 and
16 bring hope. First, God says Christians are no
longer servants when they choose Him, but instead
are friends! Second, God chose us to be His friends
before we thought about choosing Him!

Be excited! Jesus says we are His friends! He says
we are even more than friends; we are family —
adopted sons and daughters! His invitation to us is:
talk to Me, spend time with Me, do things with Me,
live life with Me!

## Application to Life

As you have studied this lesson, reflect on your
own relationship with God as it relates to prayer.
Which of the following reflects most closely your
current situation? (These responses are not intended
for discussion)

☐ I am satisfied with my prayer life

☐ My prayer life has peaks and valleys

☐ I need to put my prayer life in order

☐ I need to begin a prayer life

☐ I commit myself to developing a prayer life that
    allows me to stay continually connected to Jesus

## Prayer Time

As your group prays together, specifically ask God to assist the members in their prayer lives. Ask God to help them organize their schedules to spend adequate time with Him. At the end of your prayer time, read the Lord's Prayer together.

*Our Father which art in heaven. hallowed be thy name. Thy kingdom come. Thy will be done in earth, as it is in heaven. Give us this day our daily bread. And forgive us our debts, as we forgive our debtors. And lead us not into temptation, but deliver us from evil: For thine is the kingdom, and the power, and the glory for ever. Amen.*

# God Is Able

"The relations between God and each soul are as distinct and full as though there were not another soul upon the earth to share His watchcare, not another soul for whom He gave His beloved son." — E.G. White.

## Group Life

It is a mystery, yet a fantastic fact that God can have a one-to-one relationship with every person upon the earth at the same time! Imagine that the relationship between you and God can be the same as between you and your best friend. Also, as your group members spend time together each week, you will discover that the support and friendship that develops provides an example of what God wants to exist between each Christian and Himself.

Prayer time with God is like a private visit. When you want to be alone with God, where do you go? Bedroom, office, woods, car, living room?_____

## Scripture and Life

If you could ask God to grant one major request in your life, what would it be? Would you ask Him to . . . heal your body? put the pieces back together in your marriage? give you a better job or straighten out the one you have? mend a relationship between you and a son or daughter?

Write your request here:_____

_____

_____

Whatever your request might be, do you honestly believe God can or will do anything about it? How often do you talk to Him about your request?

Do you discover that you present your request to God, only to wallow in disbelief? It is one thing to believe; it is another to release a need to God.

As you continue in your journey of learning how to pray, remember that God accepts you where you are and assists you to grow in Him despite your weaknesses! An important part of growing in prayer is learning to accept God at His word — to trust our lives to Him. God invites us to release our cares to Him. Listen to His words: "Call upon me in the day of trouble: I will deliver you and you shall glorify me" (Psalm 50:15).

"He shall call upon me and I will answer him; I will be with him in trouble; I will deliver him and honour him" (Psalm 91:15).

Satan serves up for each of us a variety of troubles on the plate of life, yet the range and power of prayer is as great as any trouble, as universal as any sorrow, as infinite as any grief. Prayer connects us with an "Able God." There is no discouragement that prayer cannot relieve. There is no problem of life that prayer cannot conquer.

Acts 12:1-19 contains a story that illustrates how God is able to do anything, despite any lack of trust in His people. It is a story of power and of hope!

The story takes place several years after the death and resurrection of Jesus. The government of Judea was in the hands of Herod Agrippa; however, he was subject to Claudius, the Roman emperor. Herod was a convert to the Jewish faith and was zealous in carrying out the ceremonies of the Jewish law. Desirous of obtaining favor with the Jews, he persecuted Christians and began imprisoning and executing the leaders of the church. The story is as follows:

> 1) Now about that time Herod the king stretched out his hand to harass some from the church. 2) Then he killed James the brother of John with the sword. 3) And because He saw that it pleased the Jews, he proceeded further to seize Peter also. Now it was during the Days of Unleavened Bread. 4) So when he had apprehended him, he put him in prison, and delivered him to four squads of soldiers to keep him, intending to bring him before the people after the Passover. 5) Peter was therefore kept in prison, but constant prayer was offered to God for him by the church. 6) And when Herod was about to bring him out, that night Peter was sleeping, bound with two chains between two soldiers; and the guards before the door were keeping the prison. 7) Now behold, an angel of the Lord stood by him, and a light shone in the prison; and he struck Peter on the side and raised him up, saying, "Arise quickly!" And his chains fell off his hands. 8) Then the angel said to him, "Gird yourself and tie on your sandals"; and so he did. And he said to him, "Put on your garment and follow me." 9) So he went out and followed him, and did not know that what was done by the angel was

real, but thought he was seeing a vision. 10) When they were past the first and the second guard posts, they came to the iron gate that leads to the city, which opened to them of its own accord; and they went out and went down one street, and immediately the angel departed from him. 11) And when Peter had come to himself, he said, "Now I know for certain that the Lord has sent His angel, and has delivered me from the hand of Herod and from all the expectation of the Jewish people." 12) So, when he had considered this, he came to the house of Mary, the mother of John whose surname was Mark, where many were gathered together praying. 13) And as Peter knocked at the door of the gate, a girl named Rhoda came to answer. 14) When she recognized Peter's voice, because of her gladness she did not open the gate, but ran in and announced that Peter stood before the gate. 15) But they said to her, "You are beside yourself!" Yet she kept insisting that it was so. So they said, "It is his angel." 16) Now Peter continued knocking; and when they opened the door and saw him, they were astonished. 17) But motioning to them with his hand to keep silent, he declared to them how the Lord had brought him out of the prison. And he said, "Go, tell these things to James and to the brethren." And he departed and went to another place. 18) Then, as soon as it was day, there was no small stir among the soldiers about what had become of Peter. 19) But when Herod had searched for him and not found him, he examined the guards and commanded that they should be put to death. And he went down from Judea to Caesarea, and stayed there.

As we consider this story, let's summarize the setting.

- ♦ **Verse 1:** Herod persecutes the church.
- ♦ **Verse 2:** He decapitates the disciple James.

James and his brother John were known as the Sons of Thunder. John the brother of James wrote the Gospel of John, the epistles of John; and the book of Revelation.

♦ **Verse 3:** Peter is arrested and placed in prison, apparently in preparation for his own execution. Peter was one of the original twelve disciples of Jesus.

♦ **Verse 4:** Four squads of soldiers (16 men) are set to guard Peter so he does not escape.

**To think about:** If you were arrested by a dictatorial government for being a Christian, what evidence might be presented as proof of your guilt?_____

_____

_____

♦ **Verse 5:** The words of this verse are intriguing. Constant prayer was offered to God by Peter's Christian friends. It appears that Peter had a "small group." Do you have a group of friends you know who pray for you each day? (Yes or No)_____

❑ What is it like to know you have others praying for you?_____

_____

_____

♦ **Verses 6 and 7:** In these verses Herod does everything humanly possible to prevent Peter's escape. He chains Peter's arms to two guards and locks the men in a cell. Guards are then placed outside the cell. Sixteen men are assigned to guard Peter so that fresh, wide-awake guards can take turns on duty.

❑ Have you ever faced a problem in your life that seemed humanly impossible to solve? Describe it:

_____

_____

❑ Are you currently facing a problem in your life that appears overwhelming to you? If you feel comfortable doing so, share that problem with your group. They can then pray about that problem during the prayer time._____

_____

_____

Notice how verse 7 says that as the angel spoke, the chains fell away from Peter. Remember that man's extremity is God's opportunity!

♦ **Verses 8-17:** These verses demonstrate not only the power of God but man's unbelief. Verses 7-10 describe God's ability to make Satan's resistance seem like child's play. Resisting God is futile. God is all-powerful, and this is evident not only in His work as Creator, but in the victory over sin Christ won through His sinless life and sacrificial death.

❑ Can you remember an experience in your life when God intervened in a miraculous way, demonstrating that He Is Able? Have someone in the group share such an experience.

Notice the reaction of the early Christians to God's intervention on Peter's behalf. Review verses 8-17:

♦ **Verse 8:** The church is praying constantly and earnestly for Peter's release.

♦ **Verse 9:** Peter doesn't believe his freedom is real; he thinks he is having a vision. The normally talkative Peter is dumb with amazement.

♦ **Verses 10, 11:** The angel leaves Peter, and he finally recognizes that his freedom is real!

♦ **Verse 12:** Peter goes to a house full of praying Christians and knocks on the door.

♦ **Verses 13, 14:** Rhoda recognizes Peter and tells the others that Peter is at the door. They don't even go look! They say, "Impossible" and keep praying for his release!

♦ **Verse 16:** Peter keeps banging on the door. They go to see what the commotion is, and when they see Peter, they are "astonished." They can't believe he is free!

❑ Discuss together how you feel about how Peter, Rhoda, and the other praying church members responded to Peter's deliverance. What did their response indicate about their faith?_____

❑ Do you think the church members were sincere in their constant, earnest prayers?_____

_____

_____

❑ Why didn't the members believe that Peter was at the door? Why didn't they get off their knees to go look?_____

_____

_____

❑ How do you think you would have reacted if you had been part of that group of praying Christians?

_____

_____

❑ Are there any of your prayer requests about which you would be surprised should God answer them in the affirmative?_____

_____

_____

❑ As you reflect upon the events of this story, what does it say to you about God's ability to answer prayers?_____

_____

_____

❏ What does it say to you about your own prayer life and relationship with God?_____

_____

_____

## Application to Life

As I think about this miraculous story. . .

☐ I want to thank God for being a God who is able!

☐ I want to ask God for more trust in Him.

☐ I need to ask God to forgive me for my unbelief.

As your group prays together, remember to include the following in your prayers:

◆ Thanksgiving and praise to God for His power.

◆ Personal needs of members in the group.

◆ That each group member will grow in his or her trust in Jesus.

Promises to Remember:

◆ "I the Lord do not change." Malachi 3:6.

◆ "Jesus Christ is the same yesterday and today and forever." Hebrews 13:8.

◆ "Have you not known? Have you not heard? The everlasting God, the Lord, the Creator of the ends of the earth, neither faints nor is weary." Isaiah 40:28.

After the group prays, have members repeat the following verse together:

◆ "Now to Him who is able to do exceedingly abundantly above all that we ask or think, according to the power that works in us, to Him be glory in the church by Christ Jesus throughout all ages, world without end. Amen." Ephesians 3:20, 21.

# Jesus Our Example—Why Jesus Prayed

"Unceasing prayer is the unbroken union of the soul with God, so that life from God flows into our life; and from our life, purity and holiness flow back to God." —E.G. White.

## Group Life

We live in a fast-moving, ever-changing society—in a time that has been called the Information Age. What we learn today may be outdated tomorrow. Even new discoveries are soon overtaken by even newer ones. This "high-tech, low-touch" society can cause us to become caught up in a whirlwind of activity. We can easily lose touch with what really anchors us to God and the true meaning of life.

Many people, including Christians, are constantly seeking to devise new methods, plans, and organizational strategies. In the business world the purpose of all this is to increase profits. In the church, it is to expand and grow.

The danger is that people may fall between the cracks or get lost in analyzing data. God's plan is to make people the priority and methods secondary. People *are* God's method. The church and society are looking for better methods. God is looking for better people.

❑ In order to be a part of God's method — to become a person of prayer — what needs to change in your life? What might need to be eliminated or added to your daily schedule?_____

_____

_____

## Scripture and Life

♦ Jesus was a man of prayer. No one on earth has ever had a job assignment more important than His, but He always took time to pray.

♦ Jesus had a mission to accomplish — a mission that centered on eternal issues of life and death — but He took time to pray.

♦ Jesus had the power to heal the sick and raise the dead — but He took time to pray.

♦ Jesus had an agenda that overshadows that of any earthly leader — but He took time to pray.

♦ Jesus made prayer a priority. His life was focused on prayer.

Have you ever wondered why Jesus prayed? Why did He take so much of His valuable 24-hour day in talking with God the Father? This lesson will address this question and help us focus on the priority of prayer.

The following Scriptures summarize Jesus' life of prayer:

♦ "And when He had sent the multitudes away, He went up on a mountain by Himself to pray. And when evening had come, He was alone there." Matthew 14:23.

♦ "Now in the morning, having risen a long while before daylight, He went out and departed to a solitary place; and there He prayed." Mark 1:35.

♦ "And when He had sent them away, He departed to the mountain to pray. Mark 6:46.

♦ "Now when all the people were baptized, it came to pass that Jesus also was baptized; and while He prayed, the heaven was opened. And the Holy Spirit descended in bodily form like a dove upon Him." Luke 3:21, 22.

♦ "And it happened as He was alone praying, that His disciples joined Him." Luke 9:18.

❑ As you consider these verses, what do they say to you about the priority of prayer in Jesus' life?

_____

_____

❑ What time of the day did Jesus pray?_____

_____

❑ Is there any time of the day that is better for prayer than another?_____

_____

❑ Let's now get more specific in considering the previous question. Since each of us operates on a different "biological clock," do you think that for some, certain times of the day may be better for prayer than other times?_____

_____

❑ One question that can arise as we consider the example of Christ's own prayer life is this: Why did Jesus pray? If He was both God and man, why did He pray to God the Father? Spend a few moments discussing this issue and summarize the results here:_____

_____

_____

_____

If your group wishes to study the above question in greater depth, the following references will provide assistance and insights: John 1, John 17:1-5, John 14:7-11, Romans 5:12-21, Philippians 2:5-8, and Matthew 1:18-25.

Note: One of the reasons Jesus came to this earth was to demonstrate that through a relationship with God, it is possible to overcome sin. By His example, Jesus demonstrated how this could be accomplished. The source of His strength was divine power, available through His constant prayer connection with His Father.

Additional Notes:

_____

_____

_____

_____

_____

As we focus on the need for daily prayer, consider an example in Jesus' life that demonstrates the necessity of prayer, as recorded in Matthew 26:36-46.

36) Then Jesus came with them to a place called Gethsemane, and said to the disciples, "Sit here while I go and pray over there." 37) And He took with Him Peter and the two sons of Zebedee, and He began to be sorrowful and deeply distressed. 38) Then He said to them, "My soul is exceedingly sorrowful, even to death. Stay here and watch with Me." 39) He went a little farther and fell on His face, and prayed, saying, "O My Father, if it is possible, let this cup pass from Me, nevertheless, not as I will, but as You will." 40) Then He came to the disciples and found them asleep, and said to Peter, "What, could you not watch with Me one hour? 41) Watch and pray, lest you enter into temptation. The spirit indeed is willing, but the flesh is weak." 42) He went away again a second time and prayed, saying, "O My Father, if this cup cannot pass away from Me unless I drink it, Your will be done." 43) And He came and found them asleep again, for their eyes were heavy. 44) So He left them, went away again, and prayed the third time, saying the same words. 45) Then He came to His disciples and said to them, "Are you still sleeping and resting? Behold, the hour is at hand, and the Son of Man is being betrayed into the hands of sinners. 46) Rise, let us be going. See, he who betrays Me is at hand."

## Verses 36-38:

❑ Gethsemane was a garden or park-like area near

Jerusalem. The crucifixion is hours away, and
Christ's death is imminent. Jesus and His twelve
disciples retreat to Gethsemane to pray. Jesus is
obviously overwhelmed with emotion (verse 37
says He is "sorrowful and troubled"). He asks
Peter, James, and John (the two sons of Zebedee) to
pray with Him alone. What emotions do you
believe Jesus was feeling? Why?_____

_____

_____

## Verses 37, 40, 41:

❑ Jesus asked the disciples to "watch" with Him.
What does it mean to "watch"?_____

_____

_____

❑ Why did He ask the disciples to "watch"?_____

_____

_____

❑ Why was it necessary for Jesus to pray in order to
receive strength? Why didn't He just let His own
divine nature take over?_____

_____

_____

## Verses 39, 42:

❑ What is Jesus' request of the Father? What is the meaning of the word "cup"?_____

_____

_____

❑ What conditions ("ifs") does Jesus include in His request to the Father—and why?_____

_____

_____

❑ How does Christ's prayer in this passage provide a model for our own prayers?_____

_____

_____

## Verses 40, 43, 45:

❑ Why did Jesus want the disciples to pray with Him?_____

_____

❑ Why do you think the disciples could not stay awake?

☐ They did not understand Jesus' need.

☐ They were tired from overwork.

☐ They did not care.

☐ Their prayer life was not as developed as Jesus'.

☐ Other_____

## Application to Life

❑ What has been your "Gethsemane" — the place in your experience where you have wrestled with God?_____

_____

_____

_____

If you can be comfortable in doing so, share your Gethsemane experience with your group.

❑ What do you learn from Jesus' example of praying at these difficult times?_____

_____

_____

❑ Who might you want to pray with you if you faced a personal "Gethsemane"?_____

_____

❑ What have you learned most about yourself from this story? About Jesus?_____

_____

_____

_____

In the introduction, we discovered that Jesus made prayer a priority. He was not so busy doing good for others that He did not take time to pray. A trap of Satan is to get Christians so busy working for Jesus that they forget to pray. As activity increases and success is seen in God's work, there is a danger in trusting human plans and methods. There is a tendency to pray less and have less faith. Reflect on the question with which this study guide began: What needs to change in your life for prayer to be a priority? Take several minutes alone and write down three things you can do—and for which you seek God's assistance—to make prayer a priority in your life.

1._____

2._____

3._____

## Prayer Time

Pray for God specifically to answer the prayer-list requests of each group member. Remember that these lists are personal and it is not necessary for group members to share their lists. However, if someone wishes to share items from his or her list, that is permissible.

# Answered Prayer

"Real prayer helps God and man. God's kingdom is advanced by it. The greatest good comes to man by it. Prayer can do anything that God can do. The pity is that we do not believe this as we ought, and we do not put it to the test." — E.M. Bounds.

Note: Lessons 5 and 6 form a unit, in which the subjects of "Answered Prayer" and "Why Prayers Aren't Answered" will be studied. This lesson focuses on God's desire to hear and honor the prayers of His people. Lesson 6 will discuss conditions to answered prayer.

## Group Life

Most of us as children stood beside a wishing pond and stared at all the pennies, nickels, dimes, and quarters lying at the bottom. Our thoughts probably ranged from, "I would sure like to have all that money!" to "I wonder how many of the wishes represented by those coins ever came true?"

❑ God, of course, is not like a wishing pond or a

55

Santa Claus — though some think He should be.
But He is interested in what interests you and me.
If you could ask God to do one thing for you or for
someone special to you, what would you request?

_____

_____

_____

## Scripture and Life

When you pray, do you believe that God will answer
every prayer? Do you expect an answer to every
prayer? In a previous lesson, we studied the prayer life
of Jesus. Not only did Jesus illustrate in His life how
prayer works, He also had a lot to say about the topic,
as indicated in such verses as the following:

♦ "If you abide in Me, and My words abide in
  you, you will ask what you desire, and it shall
  be done for you." John 15:7.

♦ "And Jesus lifted up His eyes and said, "Father, I
  thank You that You have heard Me. And I know
  that You always hear Me, but because of the
  people who are standing by I said this, that they
  may believe that you sent Me." John 13:41, 42.

♦ "And whatever you ask in My name, that I
  will do, that the Father may be glorified in the
  Son. If you ask anything in My name, I will do
  it." John 14:13, 14.

♦ "And all things what ever you ask in prayer,
  believing, you will receive." Matthew 21:22.

As we can see, God enjoys answering prayer for
His people. Prayer, of course, does not consist only of
asking. It also includes praise, thankfulness,

acknowledgment, and glorifying God. However, petitioning and making requests to God is a significant part of prayer.

Some Christians, however, approach God timidly in prayer. They fear "making demands" of God, so sometimes Bible promises are only halfheartedly claimed.

These Bible promises are the ground on which faith stands in making requests of God. That is why the prophets could boldly approach Him.

❏ Do you think the promises quoted earlier in this section are guaranteed "blank checks" from God which we may present to Him in prayer?

_____

_____

_____

❏ Are you comfortable in claiming Bible promises as you make your own prayer requests? Why, or why not?_____

_____

_____

❏ 1 John 5:14 says that we must claim God's promises in accordance with God's will. But how can we know God's will? And how long must we wait after we have prayed, to find out what His will is?_____

_____

_____

❑ When we present a request to God in prayer, what
are His options in responding?_____

_____

_____


❑ When God apparently says "No" or "Not now,"
how does it make you feel about Him?_____

_____

_____


❑ Will every prayer request ultimately receive a
positive answer? And will we eventually think
positively about a negative answer?_____

_____

_____

_____


❑ Are there any Bible promises you can claim that
you can *know* are definitely God's will—and that
you can thus claim, knowing already that God's
answer is Yes? If so, list some of these promises:

_____

_____

_____

_____

_____

God explicitly says in Jeremiah 33:3: "Call unto me, and I will answer." There are no limitations, no hindrances in the way of God fulfilling this promise. His word is at stake. As God's people, we are to:

♦ Look for the answer.

♦ Expect the answer.

♦ With humble boldness, thank Him for the answer before we see it.

An excellent example of this is found in I Kings 18. The major characters in the story here are God, Elijah, Ahab, Jezebel, and the prophets of Baal. The Israelite nation, led by King Ahab and his wife Jezebel, are pagan worshipers. The two leaders have led Israel to worship the false god, Baal. In order to cause Israel to realize their mistake and return to Him, God works dramatically through the prophet Elijah.

God tells Elijah to let King Ahab and the Israelites know that there will be a drought in Israel. For three years, there is no rain. The rivers and streams dry up. There is no food to eat. Because of this, Ahab and Jezebel are searching for Elijah to kill him.

After three years, Elijah comes out of hiding. He appears to Ahab and sets up a showdown between God and Baal. Two altars are built, and the sacrifice of a bull is placed on each. Elijah has water poured over God's altar to enhance the challenge. Ahab and Elijah call upon their gods to ignite their sacrifices with fire.

We pick up the story in 1 Kings 18:36-46:

36) And it came to pass, at the time of the offering of the evening sacrifice, that Elijah the prophet came near and said, "Lord God of Abraham, Isaac, and Israel, let it be known this day that You are God in Israel, and that I am Your servant, and that I have

done all these things at Your word. 37) "Hear me, O
Lord, hear me, that this people may know that You
are the Lord God, and that You have turned their
hearts back to You again." Then the fire of the Lord
fell and consumed the burnt sacrifice, and the wood
and the stones and the dust, and it licked up the
water that was in the trench. 38) Now when all the
people saw it, they fell on their faces; and they said,
"The Lord, He is God! The Lord, He is God!" 40)
And Elijah said to them, "Seize the prophets of Baal!
Do not let one of them escape!" So they seized them;
and Elijah brought them down to the Brook Kishon
and executed them there. 41) Then Elijah said to
Ahab, "Go up, eat and drink; for there is the sound
of abundance of rain." 42) So Ahab went up to eat
and drink. And Elijah went up to the top of Carmel;
then he bowed down on the ground, and put his face
between his knees, 43) and said to his servant, "Go
up now, look toward the sea." So he went up and
looked, and said, "There is nothing." And seven times
he said, "Go again." 44) Then it came to pass the
seventh time, that he said, "There is a cloud, as small
as a man's hand, rising out of the sea!" So he said, "Go
up, say to Ahab, 'Prepare your chariot, and go down
before the rain stops you.'" 45) Now it happened in the
meantime that the sky became black with clouds and
wind, and there was a heavy rain. So Ahab rode away
and went to Jezreel. 46) Then the hand of the Lord
came upon Elijah; and he girded up his loins and ran
ahead of Ahab to the entrance of Jezreel.

## Verses 36, 37:

Was Elijah's prayer . . .

☐ presumption?

☐ based on faith?

☐ a chance — what if God doesn't produce?

☐ other?_____

❑ Based on these verses, what was the reason for Elijah's prayer?_____

_____

_____

❑ Elijah boldly approached God. Do you think you have the faith to pray as he did? Do you think the fact Elijah was a prophet put him in a different category than the "common, everyday Christian" in getting answers to his prayers?_____

_____

_____

_____

## Verse 39:

❑ Do you think the people responded to God because of fear—or out of true respect and devotion?_____

_____

_____

❑ When God acts dramatically in your life, how do you respond to Him? Is your response short term or long term?_____

_____

_____

## Verses 41-44:

These verses are intriguing. Elijah prays for rain.

Before there is a cloud in the sky, he tells Ahab to go to town before the "downpour" begins.

❑ What impresses you the most about these verses?

_____

_____

❑ When the servant is sent seven times to look for clouds, is this pressing God for an answer?_____

_____

_____

❑ Why do you think it took "seven looks" before a cloud appeared?_____

_____

_____

❑ Do you see any differences between how you pray and how Elijah prayed? What are they?_____

_____

_____

_____

## Application to Life

Faith such as Elijah's is needed in the lives of Christians today—a faith that will hold fast to the promises of God's Word and refuse to let go until heaven hears. Faith such as this connects us closely with heaven and brings strength for coping with the powers of Satan.

❑ If you could ask God to do one thing for you to improve your prayer life, what would it be?

☐ Change your daily schedule to allow more time to pray.

☐ Give you more faith.

☐ Give you boldness to approach God.

☐ Teach you perseverance in prayer.

☐ Other_____

## Prayer Time

In your prayer time together as a group, have someone pray specifically by name for the prayer life of each group member. Remember to keep your prayers short, in order to give everyone who wishes an opportunity to pray. And remember that praying should be totally voluntary. Close by repeating the Lord's Prayer together.

# Obstacles to Answered Prayer

"There is no time or place in which it is inappropriate to offer up a petition to God. There is nothing that can prevent us from lifting up our hearts in the spirit of earnest prayer." —E.G. White.

## Group Life

I am acquainted with a teacher who is the proud parent of a three-year-old son. The toddler has grown up, in his brief years of life, as a "gymnastic baby." That translates into doing tricks with Dad that would cause most kids to shudder. The little fellow simply laughs and grins ear to ear, because he has grown up trusting his Dad. Even though some of the routines would scare most people, he knows it is OK, because he is with Dad—the one whom he trusts. Faith has developed between father and son because of experience and association together.

Jesus said that faith and childlikeness is part of the Christian life. This life includes prayer.

❏ In addition to God, is there a special friend whom you trusted while you were growing up? Who was the friend, where did you live, and what made him or her special?_____

_____

_____

_____

## Scripture and Life

This topic, for some, is the most difficult in this entire series of lessons! After we read the positive promises of what God wants to do for us in answer to prayer, someone points out the following Scriptures:

♦ "You ask and do not receive, because you ask amiss, that you may spend it on your pleasures." James 4:3.

♦ "If I regard iniquity in my heart, the Lord will not hear." Psalm 66:18.

We may also read that much prayer is vital for the Christian, but that if it is the wrong kind of prayer, it does us no good (Matthew 6:5-8). The topic can become a little confusing at first glance. However, God does talk about conditions that contribute to an effective, growing prayer life. Let's be brave and tackle the issues together.

## Issue No. 1: Realize Our Need

The first condition to answered prayer is to realize your need of God. If you have no need, there is no reason to approach God. This may seem elementary, but many — Christians included — do not fully realize their need of coming to God daily, moment by moment. The disciple John discussed this in Revelation 3:16, 17: "I will spew you out of my mouth." "Because you say, 'I am rich, have become wealthy, and have need of nothing' and do not know that you are wretched, miserable, poor, blind and naked."

If you come to God because of an honest desire to seek a relationship with Him, He listens. If you come to Him out of obligation—trying to be a checklist Christian—your prayers will probably ricochet off the ceiling instead of penetrating heaven.

❑ How does one realize his or her need of God?

_____

_____

A promise: "The one who comes to me I will by no means cast out." John 6:37.

❑ How do you know if you are being honest with God about your needs? About your sins?

_____

_____

_____

## Issue No. 2: Ask for Help by Faith

Do you remember the man who came to Jesus and told Him that his son was having severe convulsions, foaming at the mouth? Jesus said the boy would be healed if the father believed. The Bible says that "Immediately the father of the child cried out and said with tears, 'Lord, I believe; help my unbelief!'"

The father had a need. He recognized the need, and with an honest, open, and sincere heart, he depended upon Jesus. Jesus didn't give him a checklist to meet but accepted the father where he was in his life experience.

❑ Why is it difficult for some to be honest with God? Why run from Him? Doesn't He know everything anyway?_____

_____

_____

_____

❑ What did the father of the boy mean when he said, "I believe, help my unbelief"?_____

_____

_____

❑ Have you ever felt like this father?_____

_____

## Issue No. 3: Cherished Sin

This is the issue that causes many Christians to wince. "If I regard iniquity in my heart, the Lord will not hear me." Psalm 66:18.

The key to "unpacking" the message of this verse is to understand sin—especially cherished sin.

❑ Take a moment for each group member to write a definition of *sin*; then share your definitions.

_____

_____

_____

❑ Now take time for each member to write a definition of *cherished sin*; then share the definitions._____

_____

_____

_____

Points to stimulate thinking:

♦ We must not define sin only in terms of behavior or physical actions. Sin should be defined in terms of relationship with God.

♦ Our broken relationship with God causes sinful behavior. In other words, relationship is key to behavior.

♦ Sin is something for which we immediately want forgiveness—and which we desire to overcome.

♦ Cherished sin is present when we deliberately ignore God because we don't want to have the sin removed from our life.

❑ How does sin disrupt our prayer life?_____

_____

_____

## Issue No. 4: An Attitude of Forgiveness

This issue causes more than a few to wince and say "ouch!" In the Lord's Prayer, Jesus says, "Forgive us our debts [sins] as we forgive our debtors [those who sin against us]" Matthew 6:12. In other words, it is a sin for a Christian not to completely forgive others.

Sin impedes our prayer life, as we have already discovered.

❑ If someone has made you angry for a legitimate reason (such as stealing, abuse, murder, assault, rape, kidnapping, unfaithfulness in marriage, slander, and so on) how do you overcome the desire for revenge rather than forgiving?_____

_____

_____

❑ Is it possible to forgive and still be angry?_____

_____

_____

❑ How do you forgive and forget? Can you really forget?_____

_____

Jesus went to the heart of the matter of forgiveness when He said in Matthew 5:23, "Therefore if you bring your gift to the altar, and there remember that your brother has something against you, leave your gift there before the altar, and go your way. First be reconciled to your brother, and then come and offer your gift."

❑ The responsibility of reconciliation rests with even the innocent party—not just the guilty one. Why do you think Jesus stated this principle of reconciliation?_____

❏ A question to consider privately: Is there a personal relationship that needs healing in your life that is hindering your relationship with Jesus?

Have the group take a moment and silently release these issues to God in prayer.

### Issue No. 5: Perseverance in Prayer

A previous lesson explored this issue in depth; however, a brief review may be helpful. One scripture which anchors this point is Philippians 4:6: "Be anxious for nothing, but in everything by prayer and supplication, with thanksgiving, let your requests be made known to God."

*Prayer*, as mentioned in this passage, refers to prayer in a general way. *Supplication* is continually laying before God a specific need or burden that weighs upon the heart and mind.

❏ Why is it necessary to "persevere" in prayer when God hears us the first time we talk to Him?_____

_____

_____

❏ Can lack of perseverance in prayer keep our prayers from being answered? If so, when do you know that it's time to stop asking? Could this make prayer mechanical or "works" oriented?

_____

_____

_____

To think about:

♦ Could perseverance refer to being in constant

connection with God, rather than to "pressing the request"?

♦ Could perseverance mean to pray publicly, privately, at work, in the car, or at school as we would talk to a friend?

♦ Could perseverance mean to talk to God about a need or problem as much as we need to for our own peace of mind?

♦ Could it be that perseverance doesn't change God; it changes us?

## Application to Life

As you have reflected on these five issues concerning answered prayer, maybe one of them has spoken to you. If you feel comfortable in doing so, share with your group one of the areas you would like them to pray about for you.

_____

_____

My personal response:

☐ I need more fully to recognize my need of God.

☐ "I believe, help my unbelief."

☐ I want to ask God to forgive my sins and give me victory over them.

☐ I want an attitude of forgiveness toward all people.

☐ I want a continual attitude of prayer in my daily life.

## Prayer Time

In your prayer time, ask God to give all group members growth and victory in their personal lives in the areas touched on in the five issues discussed in this lesson.

Prayer activity suggestion:

The group leader, during prayer time, can mention individually the five prayer responses in the "Application to Life" section on the previous page — then pause for a moment to allow members time to pray about that response as it relates to their personal life.

Also, remember that there is hope, forgiveness, and strength in Jesus. He has won the victory for us over Satan! When we yield our lives and desires to Christ, we have the assurance of forgiveness and eternal life in Him.

"If we confess our sins, He is faithful and just to forgive us our sins and to cleanse us from all unrighteousness." 1 John 1:9.

"And this is the testimony: that God has given us eternal life, and this life is in His Son." 1 John 5:11.

# How to Pray—Part 1

"Christ's lessons in regard to prayer should be carefully considered. There is a divine science in prayer, and His illustration brings to view principles that all need to understand." —E.G. White.

## Group Life

Many people carry an appointment book in their pocket, briefcase, purse, or backpack for school—or keep one on their desk at home. This book, for many, is the "brain" that directs their daily routine. People with busy lives pencil in exercise time, family time, and other miscellaneous events. In fact, the list can be virtually endless. I wonder how many write into their schedule books a daily appointment with God.

If you are struggling with your prayer time, finding it routinely squeezed by other commitments, try writing your devotional time into your appointment book. God is, after all, the most important appointment of the day!

❑ During your lifetime so far, who is the most

famous human being with whom you have had an
appointment?_____

_____

❑ Where do you need to record or note your
   appointment time with God so that it won't be
   forgotten?_____

_____

## Scripture and Life

In Matthew 6 is the passage known as the Lord's
Prayer. These verses are memorized and repeated by
Christians worldwide. The same prayer is referred to
by other gospel writers, but in a slightly different
context. Our study in this lesson will center on this
prayer as recorded by Luke.

The context of Luke 11:1-9 sets the foundation for
Jesus' teaching on how to pray. Jesus and His
disciples had recently arrived at the town of Bethany,
located outside of Jerusalem on the Mount of Olives.
Mary, Martha, and Lazarus (brother and sisters) lived
together in Bethany, and Jesus stopped by for a visit.
Possibly one evening or morning, Jesus went into the
garden behind the house to pray. The disciples had
watched and listened as Christ prayed on earlier
occasions. This particular time, they said, "Lord,
teach us to pray."

1) And it came to pass, as He was praying in a
certain place, when He ceased, that one of His
disciples said to Him, "Lord, teach us to pray, as
John also taught his disciples." 2) So He said to
them, "When you pray, say: Our Father in heaven,
Hallowed be Your name. Your kingdom come. Your
will be done. On earth as it is in heaven. 3) Give us
day by day our daily bread. 4) And forgive us our

sins, For we also forgive everyone who is indebted to us. And do not lead us into temptation, But deliver us from the evil one." 5) And He said to them, "Which of you shall have a friend, and go to him, saying, 'Friend, lend me three loaves; 6) for a friend of mine has come to me on his journey, and I have nothing to set before him;' 7) and he will answer from within and say, 'Do not trouble me; the door is now shut, and my children are with me in bed; I cannot rise and give to you'? 8) I say to you, though he will not rise and give to him because he is his friend, yet because of his persistence he will rise and give him as many as he needs. 9) And I say to you, ask, and it will be given to you; seek, and you will find; knock, and it will be opened to you."

This passage teaches us the basic principles of how to pray and what to include in those prayers. Jesus did not give a specific list or order to pray through which must be followed if our prayer is to be valid. He did, however, suggest in this prayer certain things we should pray about.

## Principle No. 1: Acknowledge God as Supreme

*"Our Father in Heaven"*

❑ List and discuss the points that come to your mind as you compare an earthly parent with God.

_____

_____

_____

_____

_____

❑ Why is it important for us to acknowledge God's sovereignty or leadership over us?_____

_____

_____

## Principle No. 2: Give Praise and Thanks to God

*"Hallowed be Your name"*

❑ Why is it necessary to verbally give praise and thanks to God?_____

_____

_____

❑ For what should we praise and thank Him?_____

_____

_____

_____

❑ Which of the following help you most in expressing your praise to and reverence for God?

☐ Worship services
☐ Music
☐ Prayers
☐ Quoting scriptures of praise
☐ Obedience to His Word
☐ Showing love and kindness to others
☐ Performing a ministry for Him

## Principle No. 3: An Attitude of Expectation

*"Your Kingdom come"*

❑ To Christians, God provides hope and the promise of better living conditions later on. Does the phrase, "Your Kingdom come" create in you a sense of expectancy? If so, what is it to which you most look forward?_____

_____

_____

❑ Reflection: When the Kingdom comes, will the new life it brings meet all the needs and hopes of Christians? (Yes or No—and if Yes, how?)_____

_____

_____

## Principle No. 4: Do Not Pray Selfishly

*"Your will be done on earth as it is in heaven"*

This verse discusses our need to submit our lives and our decisions to God. It urges us to give to God our will and desires, granting Him permission to do whatever is necessary in our lives to fulfill His will.

❑ How can we know God's will concerning given questions or decisions in our lives?_____

_____

_____

_____

❑ What is the difference between a selfish and non-selfish prayer?_____

_____

_____

## Principle No. 5: Present Your Daily Personal Needs

*"Give us day by day our bread"*

This phrase confirms that it is acceptable to talk to God about our personal needs. However, in Matthew 6:25, Jesus said, "Do not worry about your life, what you will eat or what you will drink; nor about your body, what you will put on. Is not life more than food and the body more than clothing?"

❑ If God promises in Matthew to provide our needs, do we still need to ask Him for the things we need? If so, why?_____

_____

_____

❑ When Jesus said that life is more than food and clothing, what do you think He meant?_____

_____

_____

❑ Why is it important for us to remember that it is God who gives us power to get wealth? (Deuteronomy 8:18.)_____

_____

## Principle No. 6: Confess Your Sins and Ask for Forgiveness

*"And forgive us our sins, for we also forgive everyone who is indebted to us"*

Admitting our mistakes and asking forgiveness of God is vitally important. By doing so, we acknowledge God's sovereignty and the plan of salvation. However, our being forgiven is dependent upon our willingness to forgive. Daily confession to God should bring to our minds relationships that need rebuilding.

❑ Why is it important to God and to us that our being forgiven is based on our willingness to forgive?_____

_____

_____

## Principle No. 7: Express Faith and Trust

*"And do not lead us into temptation, but deliver us from the evil one"*

A wording that helps clarify this phrase is, "Do not permit us to enter into temptation." When Satan tempts us, the sin is not in being tempted, but in yielding to it. We need protection against falling into sin.

This protection comes through trusting in God's strength and power. We must give our will power (choices) to God. This is easier said than done!

❑ How did Jesus withstand temptation? (See Matthew 4:1-11)_____

❏ What have you discovered in your life that assists
you in resisting temptation?_____

_____

_____

In summary, Jesus said that these seven principles
are to be part of our prayer life:

♦ Acknowledge God as supreme

♦ Give praise and thanks to God

♦ Have an attitude of expectation

♦ Do not pray selfishly

♦ Present your daily personal need

♦ Confess your sins and ask for forgiveness

♦ Express faith and trust

The next lesson will discuss practical ways of
making these principles part of your prayer life.

## Application to Life

Jesus wants us to understand that when we pray
according to the principles set forth in the Lord's
Prayer in Luke 11, God hears and honors our prayer
requests. He emphasized this point by giving the
story found in verses 5-8. Read these verses again.
Jesus then says, "Ask," "seek," "knock," and you will
receive the promised answer.

Jesus is not concerned that we follow these
principles in the precise order in which He gave
them. However, many Christians have found more
satisfaction in their prayer life by concentrating first
upon God rather than on their personal needs. If we
were to follow the seven principles as presented by
Jesus, our approach to God would be as follows.

**God First**

◆ Address God respectfully.

◆ Thank and praise Him for who He is and for what He has done.

◆ Claim and thank Him for the promise of the second coming and a better life to come.

◆ Commit your life to God's will.

**Self Last**

◆ Talk to God about your personal needs.

◆ Talk to God about your sins and temptations.

◆ Express faith and trust in Him as an all-powerful God.

## Prayer Time

In your prayer time together, follow this suggested order of praying in a conversational prayer. Have the group leader mention aloud each principle of the Lord's Prayer in order, giving members time to pray before moving on to the next principle.

# How to Pray—Part 2

"Prayer affects God in a direct manner, and has its aim and end in affecting Him. Prayer takes hold of God, and induces Him to do large things for us, whether personal or relative, temporal or spiritual, earthly or heavenly." —E.M. Bounds.

## Group Life

In our last lesson, we looked at the story Jesus told (Luke 11:5-8) about the man whose friend visited him in the middle of the night. The visitor was hungry, and the man had no food. Because of this, he went next door to his neighbor and asked for food to feed his friend.

Jesus told the story to illustrate that God is always available to us—day or night—through prayer, and that we are to be continually in prayer to Him.

❑ Can you think of a time when you had to awaken someone in the middle of the night because you needed assistance? Describe that event:_____

## Scripture and Life

This lesson is somewhat different than the others. It builds on the principles set forth in Lesson 7: "How to Pray—Part 1." Lesson 8 will suggest practical ways of approaching God in prayer that can help make your prayer life more meaningful.

Matthew 6:5-8 discusses specifically the attitude we should have when we approach God. Also in these verses, Jesus discusses two types of prayer.

> 5) "And when you pray, you shall not be like the hypocrites. For they love to pray standing in the synagogues and on the corners of the streets, that they may be seen by men. Assuredly, I say to you, they have their reward. 6) But you, when you pray, go into your room, and when you have shut your door, pray to your Father who is in the secret place; and your Father who sees in secret will reward you openly. 7) But when you pray, do not use vain repetitions as the heathen do. For they think that they will be heard for their many words. 8) Therefore do not be like them. For your Father knows the things you have need of before you ask Him."

The two types of prayer mentioned here are public, and private. The settings in which we pray can be divided under these two types. Consider the following examples, and then on the blank lines add any others that come to your mind:

### Public prayer

♦ Church worship services

♦ Beginning of a meeting or club

♦ Church board or committee meetings

♦ Prayers at meals for a large group of people

_____

_____

_____

_____

**Private prayer**

♦ Personal devotions

♦ Prayer with one's spouse

♦ Prayer at meals

♦ Prayer at bedtime

_____

_____

_____

_____

_____

❑ Verse 5 discusses public prayers. What principles regarding prayer in public do you find in this passage?_____

_____

_____

❑ Verse 6 discusses private prayer. Why is private prayer necessary?_____

_____

_____

❏ What do you think is the primary message of verse 6?

_____

_____

❏ Verse 7 talks about our attitude in prayer and the words we use. What message from Jesus do you hear in these verses?_____

_____

_____

❏ Why is it difficult for some people to pray publicly or in a small-group setting?_____

_____

_____

❏ What can someone do who has difficulty praying with a spouse, children, or close friends?_____

_____

_____

❏ How do you react to verse 8?
  ☐ A promise from God.
  ☐ God understands me no matter what.
  ☐ Why pray?
  ☐ Other_____

Many suggestions could be offered for improving our prayer life. Some are presented here. It is possible that the following list may not include some of your own ideas. However, after this list, your group members will have an opportunity to share the ideas they have found helpful.

## Personal Devotions

General suggestions:

♦ Choose a designated daily time to meet with God. Write it in your appointment book. Fix the time firmly in your mind. If your primary devotional time is not when you first get up in the morning, remember nonetheless to make contact with God first thing in the day. And make sure to set aside enough time.

♦ Set a specific minimum amount of time for your daily appointment with God. This may vary, depending upon your circumstances. At times it may increase—or emergencies may reduce it. On holidays, vacations, and days off, plan on spending extra time with God.

♦ Choose a regular location where you can meet with God. It may be your office, sewing room, or bedroom. Select a place where interruptions can be kept to a minimum.

Other ideas:

Most people who enjoy successful devotional lives have a plan that assists them in their personal prayer and study time. Most of these plans involve a Bible, pen or pencil, paper, notebook (the size of your choice), and an outline. Consider the following ideas:

♦ Write on four separate pages in a notebook the headings of the acronym ACTS:

    ● Adoration

    ● Confession

- Thanksgiving
- Supplication

As you pray, list items on the pages under each heading. Note the dates of significant responses to your prayer requests or concerns. Under each heading, pray, sing songs, and quote verses of Scripture.

♦ Lay the Bible before you on your chair or bed. Read the passage on your knees. Pray through each verse. Apply the verse to your life in prayer as you talk to God. Have a pen or pencil and paper nearby to write down thoughts that come to you as you pray. Some especially enjoy using the prayers in the Psalms in this manner

♦ Purchase a pocket-sized notebook to which pages can be added. Divide it into the following sections:

- Praise and Thanks
- Dedication and Commitment
- Daily Needs and Requests
- Answered Prayers
- Special Victories

Under each section, list the items that come to your mind. Again, praying, singing songs, and quoting Scripture are helpful.

♦ Follow the outline of the Lord's Prayer explored in Lesson 7 during your prayer time:

- Acknowledge God for who He is.
- Praise and thankfulness.
- Commitment of self/will power and expectation to God.

- Present personal needs and concerns.

- Confession and repentance.

- Expressions of faith and trust.

Again Scripture, songs, and prayer can be listed under each section.

♦ Prayer journaling. Purchase a spiral notebook and write your thoughts and feelings to God. This helps you to focus on your feelings. Also, writing down your joys and disappointments assists in bringing healing as you empty yourself before God. An excellent book on prayer journaling, available from the publisher of this book, is *A New Way to Pray*, by Dwight K. Nelson.

♦ Several notebooks available at Christian bookstores are designed to assist Christians in their daily devotions. One such notebook—*My Partner*, by Becky Tirabassi—is divided into two sections: "My Part," and "God's Part." Under "My Part" are the following divisions:

- P = prayers of Praise

- A = prayers of Admission of sin

- R = prayers of Request

- T = prayers of Thanks to God

"God's Part" is divided as follows:

- L = Listening (a time of silence and meditation on Scripture)

- M = Messages (notes from sermons, other books, and so on)

- N = New Testament (list helpful verses from the New Testament)

- O = Old Testament (list helpful verses from the Old Testament)

- P = Proverbs  (list helpful verses from Proverbs)

The last section — "To Do" — is for making notes, lists, and schedules to help organize life as God suggests during daily devotions.

As you can see, many ideas are available for structuring and getting the most out of our daily devotional time.

Now write down any additional ideas your group members can share that have been helpful in their own personal devotions.

_____

_____

_____

_____

## Public Prayer

The reason public or group prayer is difficult for some is found in one word — FEAR. Fear that we will stumble in our choice of words. Fear that our words won't be as sophisticated or smoothly stated as those of people who have already prayed. Fear that we will embarrass ourselves. Fear that because others are better Christians, we can't pray as well. Fear that our speaking ability in prayer will be judged by others who are listening. I am sure each of us could add to this list.

Did you notice that in our list of fears, they all center on self? That our focus is on self rather God? It is true that not everyone is a public speaker, but as

Christians, there are times we need to pray for someone or in a small-group setting. Let's consider some ideas to help make public praying easier.

♦ Claim the promise of 2 Timothy 1:7: "The Lord has not given us a spirit of fear, but of power and of love and of a sound mind." This verse says that if we ask, God will replace our fear with the power of the Holy Spirit, with love for those for whom we pray, and with a peaceful mind that knows Jesus is with us.

♦ Admit your fears aloud to your Christian friends with whom you are comfortable. Ask them to pray for you, help you, and accept you in your struggle. Remember that 99 percent of Christians have felt or feel as you do. You are normal!

♦ Think of and list the various kinds of public prayers you could be asked to pray — prayers such as those during a worship service, at the beginning of a Bible Study group or board meeting, at a meal, or at the close of a meeting. Write out a prayer you might use. Read it aloud. Writing out the prayer will help you focus your mind on what to say. Then, when asked to pray, your mind will remember what you have thought about. Remember too that those listening to your prayer are your Christian friends, joining you in talking to God.

Small-group prayer suggestions:

♦ Let members know that it is fine to:

  ● Write out prayers. In fact, sometimes it can be enjoyable to have everyone in the group write out a prayer and read it.

  ● Pray conversationally — that is, to speak short

prayers as often as you want during a group prayer session.

- Pray conversationally by topics. For example, pray prayers of thanks and praise. Pray for needs outside the group. Pray for needs within the group. The group leader tells the group what topic to pray about and when to move on to the next topic.

❑ Share ideas that have assisted you in praying in public._____

_____

_____

_____

Remember: The Holy Spirit will assist you both in overcoming fear and in growing daily in your prayer life.

## Application to Life

☐ I commit myself to a daily prayer appointment with God.

☐ I commit myself to asking God's assistance in praying publicly with and for others.

☐ I need God to remove my fears about prayer.

☐ I am thankful for prayer.

☐ I am thankful for my Christian friends.

If you choose, write here the details of your personal prayer appointment with God.

♦ Time:_____

♦ Location:_____

♦ What I will do during my prayer time:_____

## Prayer Time

In your group's prayer time, have all members write out a one-sentence prayer about something for which they are thankful. If they choose, during the prayer time have group members spontaneously read their sentence. Remember that it is fine not to pray or not to read your prayer. Group members accept and respect each other at all times. Close by saying or reading the Lord's Prayer together.

Author's note: As a Christian and as a minister, I don't always pray in each group setting. There are times when my need is to be quiet and reflective. Some group members, by personality, are more quiet and reserved. This is fine. God has made each of us to be unique.

# Listening in Prayer

"When every other voice is hushed, and in quietness we wait before Him, the silence of the soul makes more distinct the voice of God. He bids us, 'Be still and know that I am God' (Psalm 46:10)." —E.G. White.

## Group Time

If your group is similar to most, some members love to talk, and others like to quietly listen, squeezing in an occasional comment. A lot of this, of course, is based on personality. However, it is important for each member both to speak and to listen. Spiritual growth takes place when there is a balance between sharing our own ideas and learning from other's ideas.

❑ It is hard work to really listen to others. When you were (or maybe you still are) between the ages of 5 and 20, did you have someone who would genuinely listen to you? If so, who was it? Why were they someone you could easily talk to? How was this like God?

## Scripture and Life

Have you ever been a prisoner of circumstances
with someone who talked too much for your liking at
that particular time? It might have been in a
meeting—or on a trip by car, bus, or plane. But you
wished your talkative companion would take a deep
breath and become reflective. Do you suppose God
ever feels that way about us—His children—
wondering if we will ever listen?

If prayer is a two-way conversation between God
and the one praying, then somewhere in the
conversation, God must be allowed some time to speak.

God has spoken and speaks now to His people in
various ways. Here are some of the ways God has
spoken—or speaks today—to His followers:

♦ He spoke to Adam and Eve face to face (Genesis
   3:8, 9).

♦ He sent angels (Genesis 19:1).

♦ He spoke through visions and dreams
   (Matthew 1:20).

♦ He spoke in an audible voice (Matthew 3:17).

♦ He used signs and symbols (Luke 2:12).

♦ He spoke through Jesus (John 3:16).

♦ He spoke through the Holy Spirit (John
   14:16-18).

♦ He speaks through the circumstances of life
   (Matthew 5:38-42).

♦ He speaks through people (Romans 10:14, 15).

♦ He speaks through silence (Psalm 46:10).

♦ He speaks through the Bible (2 Timothy 2:16, 17).

♦ He speaks through nature (Psalm 19:1).

❑ Which of the above methods has God used most often to speak to you personally?_____

_____

Since God speaks to us in different ways, this lesson will focus on the topic of meditating upon God. Read the following Scriptures, noticing the use of the word *meditation.*

♦ "Let the words of my mouth and the meditation of my heart be acceptable in your sight, O Lord, my strength and my redeemer." Psalm 19:14.

♦ "But his delight is in the law of the Lord, and in His law he meditates day and night." Psalm 1:2.

♦ "My mouth shall speak wisdom, and the meditation of my heart shall bring understanding." Psalm 49:3.

♦ Paul spoke to Timothy about the evidence of the Holy Spirit in his life and of the power God had given to him. Then he said, "Meditate on these things; give yourself entirely to them, that your progress may be evident to all." 1 Timothy 4:15.

♦ "You will keep him in perfect peace, whose mind is stayed on you, because he trusts in You." Isaiah 26:3.

♦ "Be still and know that I am God." Psalm 46:10.

The word *meditation* is a biblical word. However, some Christians shy away from it because Satan has perverted its use. Satan does this with everything that comes from God. He knows that if he can turn our minds away from anything God has created for a useful purpose, he wins. Forget the non-Christian use of the word *meditation*. Focus instead on what God has to say about it.

❑ How would you define meditation?_____

_____

_____

Meditation, or listening, requires that our minds be focused on God. As God defines it, meditation has a purpose. It is not simply putting the mind silently into neutral.

❑ Based on the verses about meditation which we just reviewed, what is its purpose?_____

_____

_____

❑ Where, according to these verses, is the mind to be focused during meditation?_____

_____

❑ What are the benefits of meditation?_____

_____

_____

Consider this definition: Meditation is the act of silently contemplating or reflecting upon God and on what He is telling me through a specific Scripture.

This Scripture message may come to me directly from the Bible, through another person, or as God inspires my mind by the Holy Spirit.

❏ Are you comfortable with this definition of meditation? (Yes or No)_____

❏ How would you change the definition?_____

_____

_____

❏ Why is it important for us to meditate or listen to God speak?_____

_____

_____

Note: As you listen quietly to God, have a paper and pen with you to jot down thoughts that come to your mind.

❏ Which would nurture your faith more?

☐ Meditation on creation

☐ Meditation on Scripture

☐ A combination of both

## Scripture Memorization

Another way of allowing God to speak to us and to impact our lives is to memorize Scripture. In Psalm 119:11, we read: "Your word I have hidden in my heart, that I might not sin against you."

❏ What does it mean to hide God's Word in the heart?_____

_____

❑ How does memorizing Scripture assist us in meditating on God?_____

_____

_____

❑ What methods have your group members found helpful in memorizing Scripture?_____

_____

_____

_____

Suggestions:

♦ Write down your favorite Scriptures on 3 by 5 cards.

♦ Carry the cards in your pocket or purse.

♦ Memorize these scriptures while driving, standing in lines, shaving, putting on makeup, waiting for appointments, and so on.

♦ Memorize with another family member or friend — the encouragement is helpful.

♦ Perhaps your group would like to memorize several Scriptures together.

## Application to Life

Genesis 5:22-24 is one of the most intriguing passages in the Bible. It tells us about a man by the name of Enoch. Enoch was a prophet, and he developed such a close walk with God that something special happened to him. Listen to the Bible:

"Enoch walked with God three hundred years and begat sons and daughters. So all the days of Enoch were three hundred and sixty-five years. And Enoch walked with God; and he was not, for God took him." The Scriptures state that Enoch walked with God and developed such a close relationship that he did not die! God took him directly to heaven! The Bible does not tell us specifically what Enoch's walk with God was like. More than likely, though, it included meditation and prayer. As you reflect upon your own relationship with God, check off your answers to the following statements.

☐ I want to live eternally with God like Enoch.

☐ I want to commit or recommit my life to Jesus as I look forward to His return to this earth.

☐ I am going to plan for times of meditation in my daily schedule.

☐ I commit myself to daily Scripture memorization.

☐ I want my group members to pray for me to grow in my prayer life.

These responses are meant to be private. However, if you or any of your fellow group members want to share one or more of these responses, you are encouraged to do so.

## Prayer Time

As your group prays together, specifically ask God to assist every member as they seek to improve their prayer relationship with Him. Ask for volunteers to pray for the entire group in relation to the statements of commitment just noted.

# Moving Mountains

"God is waiting to be put to the test by His people in prayer. He delights in being put to the test on His promises. It is His highest pleasure to answer prayer to prove the reliability of His promises. Nothing worthy of God nor of great value to men will be accomplished till this is done." —E.M. Bounds.

## Group Life

Jesus spoke many times about trust or faith. In fact, it was one of the key themes He laid down for us to contemplate and understand. These terms are so commonly used that—like the word *love*—they are defined in many ways.

As your group has spent a number of weeks together, you have probably noticed a bonding taking place between group members. This deepening of friendships includes trust in one another.

❑ Not includng God, who on earth have you trusted the most? What made this person trustworthy?_____

## Scripture and Life

It is Monday morning. Jesus and His twelve disciples are leaving the town of Bethany, on the Mount of Olives, heading to Jerusalem. Jesus is hungry. Seeing a fig tree in full leaf, He says, "Let us go see if there are figs on the tree." Even though it is not the season for figs, a tree usually does not leaf out before the fruit is formed and developed. Leaves normally mean fruit.

Upon arriving at the tree, Jesus searches its branches from top to bottom and finds no figs. The tree is a fraud. Jesus looks at the tree and declares, "Let no one eat fruit from you ever again."

Jesus and His disciples arrive at Jerusalem. After the cleansing of the temple, they spend the night in Jerusalem. The next morning, Tuesday, Jesus heads back to Bethany. One the way back, the group passes the fig tree Jesus had cursed the day before. We pick up the remainder of the story in Mark 11:20-24:

> 20) Now in the morning, as they passed by, they saw the fig tree dried up from the roots. 21) And Peter, remembering, said to Him, "Rabbi, look! The fig tree which You cursed has withered away." 22) So Jesus answered and said to them, "Have faith in God. 23) For assuredly, I say to you, whoever says to this mountain, 'Be removed and cast into the sea' and does not doubt in his heart, but believes that those things he says will come to pass, he will have whatever he says.' 24) Therefore I say to you, whatever things you ask when you pray, believe that you receive them, and you will have them."

❑ Some have suggested that the fig tree was cursed in anger. Why do you think Jesus cursed the tree?

☐ He was angry because there was no fruit on the tree.

☐ To teach a lesson about hypocrisy. Leaves—but no fruit.

☐ To teach a lesson about God's power.

☐ As a sign of what will happen to those who reject Him.

☐ As an illustration of the Jewish nation's attitude toward Him and His Kingdom.

☐ Other:_____

## Verse 20:

❑ What is the significance of the tree being dried up by the roots?_____

_____

_____

❑ What is the parallel between the withered tree and the Christian life?_____

_____

_____

## Verses 22, 23:

Peter is literally amazed that the fig tree has withered. It's as if he is saying, "I don't believe it!" In imagination, we see him staring at Jesus as he wonders, "What will He do next?"

Immediately Jesus focuses attention away from

His own act to God's power. He draws a parallel between divine power and faith.

❑ Take a few minutes for each group member to write a personal definition of faith. Then share your definitions._____

_____

_____

_____

❑ Is there a difference between faith and trust?_____

_____

(For further study: See Hebrews 11)

Note: Faith is made up of two parts: belief and trust. We believe in God's ability to do something, and we trust that He will act. Belief is not enough. James 1:19 says that the devils believe.

## Verse 23:

❑ Define what Jesus meant by "mountain." Is He referring to literal or figurative mountains?

_____

_____

_____

❑ What are the conditions listed in this verse that—when met—will move a "mountain?"

_____

_____

❑ How do the conditions listed in this verse

correspond to the preceding note about faith?
Would you reword the note, or is it satisfactory to
you?_____

_____

_____

## Verse 24:

❑ Do you struggle in your mind with this verse? Is it
a reality in your life?        _____

_____

❑ Define the "whatever" in this verse._____

_____

_____

❑ Are there conditions to this promise?_____

_____

(For further reading: James 4:13-15; 1 John 5:14, 15)

### Application to Life

The secret of "moving mountains" through prayer
is faith. The key question for Christians is, How do
you receive faith and grow in faith?

(For further reading: Romans 10:17 and 12:3).

Paul refers to the fact that all are given a "measure
of faith" and that faith comes or increases by hearing
God's Word. In a previous lesson, on Listening, we
noticed numerous ways God uses to speak to His
people.

❑ When do we first receive the "measure of faith" that God gives to each of us?_____

_____

❑ Write down what you think it would take for you to develop "mountain moving" faith._____

_____

_____

## Prayer Time

Group prayer suggestion:

Ask God to assist group members in focusing their thoughts on Him rather than on their problems and disappointments.

Personal prayer suggestion:

Don't spend a lot of time describing your mountain to the Lord. He could describe it even better than you can! Instead, focus your attention on God – the Mountain Mover. Concentrate on His power, His faithfulness. In Joshua 3, the priests carrying the ark had to step into the Jordan River at flood stage before the waters separated. Once they moved ahead in faith (they had lived in the desert all their lives and probably couldn't swim), God gave them dry land to walk on. They believed and trusted! When our focus is correct, the mountains will move.

# Power Through Prayer

"The very powers of darkness are paralyzed by prayer. No wonder Satan tries to keep our minds fussy in active work 'till we can not think to pray'." —Oswald Chambers.

## Group Life

A friend of mine told me that a fellow Christian once shared that all his life, he had believed it was wrong to pray for the Holy Spirit. The reason for this was probably because of Satan's misuse or counterfeit of the true power of the Holy Spirit. Satan wants above all else to keep us from having a Spirit (power) filled life. Christians may have many fears in this world of sin, but being filled with the Holy Spirit should not be one of them!

❑ While you were growing up, what caused you the most fear, and why?_____

_____

## Scripture and Life

If the average Christian were asked, "Where does the power received in prayer originate?" the answer would probably be, "With God." If the question were pressed further, the response would probably be, "God gives the Holy Spirit to those who ask, and it is the Spirit who empowers us."

The relationship between prayer and possessing the power of the Holy Spirit is vital for us to understand, because the purpose of prayer is to connect us with God's power. Let's briefly explore the subject of the Holy Spirit by considering four questions:

## What is the Holy Spirit? An influence— or a Person?

What do the following verses reveal about the identity of the Holy Spirit?

♦ "However, when He the Spirit of Truth, has come, He will guide you into all truth; for He will not speak on His own authority, but whatever He hears He will speak; and He will tell you things to come. He will glorify me, for He will take of what is Mine and declare it to you. All things that the Father has are Mine. Therefore I said that He will take of Mine and declare it to you." John 16:13-15.

♦ "Baptizing them [disciples] in the name of the Father and of the Son and of the Holy Spirit." Matthew 28:19.

For further study, the following verses mention personal qualities of the Spirit: 1 Corinthians 2:10, 11, 13; 1 Corinthians 12:7-11; Romans 15:30; Acts 5:3, 4; Ephesians 4:30.

## What is the job description assigned to the Holy Spirit?

John 14:16, 17, 26; 15:26; 16:7-15; Acts 1:18.

_____

_____

_____

## When and how do we receive the Holy Spirit?

❑ What do the following texts reveal about this subject? Romans 8:8-11; Ephesians 1:13, 14; 3:4-17; 4:30; 2 Corinthians 1:21, 22: 1 John 4:13.

_____

_____

_____

## How often should we pray for the Holy Spirit?

Luke 11:9-13; 1 Corinthians 15:31.

_____

_____

This brief scriptural summary reveals that the Holy Spirit is a Person able to experience emotions much as we do — and that He is a member of the Godhead. The Spirit causes us to want to accept Jesus as our Lord and Saviour. When we are converted and accept Jesus, we are filled with the Holy Spirit. The purpose of the Holy Spirit's dwelling in us is to make us like Jesus and to empower us for ministry. Just as Jesus daily prayed to the Father for strength, so we need to ask for a constant filling of the Holy Spirit as we recommit our lives each day to Him.

The work of the Holy Spirit in developing our relationship with Jesus has been a major theme in these lessons. Filled with the Holy Spirit, we will receive the fruits of the Spirit in our lives—love, joy, peace, long-suffering, kindness, goodness, faithfulness, gentleness, and self-control. In other words, we become like Jesus in character and lifestyle.

In addition to helping us to become like Jesus, the Spirit is given through prayer to empower us for ministry. We are called to a life of prayer and service. The two cannot be separated. A man or woman of prayer will be a man or woman of action for Jesus. A praying Christian is an active Christian, and an active Christian is a praying Christian. The fruits of those who pray are seen in their use of talents, abilities, and spiritual gifts for service. As praying Christians, we will ask God to reveal to us people and situations needing our ministry.

Three chapters in the Bible concentrate on the subject of spiritual gifts. These are Ephesians 4, Romans 12, and 1 Corinthians 12. Ephesians discusses the purpose of spiritual gifts, Romans the preparation necessary to receive them, and 1 Corinthians how the gifts function in the church.

Read 1 Corinthians 12 in its entirety and then consider the following questions:

❑ How many Christians receive gifts, and what determines which gifts we receive?_____

_____

_____

❑ List the gifts discussed in 1 Corinthians 12. Briefly discuss each and its application to the local church.

_____

_____

_____

_____

_____

_____

_____

_____

_____

❑ Discuss and apply the analogy of the human body and the church body to spiritual gifts and to our individual ministries._____

_____

_____

_____

_____

❑ Define the term *spiritual gift*._____

_____

_____

❑ What do you believe are your spiritual gifts to be used in ministry? _____

_____

_____

_____

Note: If your have never filled out a questionnaire to assist you in understanding your gifts, ask your group leader for assistance. Your group may enjoy filling out a Spiritual Gifts Questionnaire together.

❑ Read Romans 12:1-6. What is the "living sacrifice" God asks of each Christian?_____

_____

## Application to Life

The Holy Spirit can bless you when you study the Bible . . . the Spirit can direct you as you use your God-given abilities in ministry . . . He can speak through you as you teach or preach from the Bible . . . but if you want a close relationship with God, in which you listen and hear Him speak to you, then you must pray. Power in the Christian life does not come from "doing good." The "doing good" is the manifestation of the power. Power only comes through intimate communion with God. There are no shortcuts.

Your response:

❏ List at least three items in your life that need to change if your prayer life is to provide you with the power of the Holy Spirit. If you are comfortable with your prayer life, then list at least three obstacles Satan attempts to throw across your path to disrupt your prayer life.

_____

_____

_____

❏ As you reflect on your own involvement in active ministry, what most needs to change in your spiritual life to make your efforts more effective?

_____

_____

❏ Write down what you plan to do to make Christian service a personal priority._____

_____

_____

## Prayer Time

◆ Pray for each group member concerning the lists they have just compiled.

◆ Ask for a continual filling of the Holy Spirit.

◆ Give God praise and thanks for the power of the Holy Spirit that He gave as a gift.

♦ Conclude by repeating/reading the Lord's Prayer together — or by reading John 17:20-26 in unison.

# LESSON 12

# Praying Women and Praying Men

"Prayer overcomes him [Satan]. It defeats his plans and himself. He cannot successfully stand before it. He trembles when some man of simple faith in God prays." —S.D. Gordon.

## Group Time

There are times in life when each of us needs the support and prayers of Christian friends. The trial and difficulty may be the result of our own wrong decisions or simply the circumstances of life. As we seek solutions and strength from God, Christian friends are necessary. True friends may disagree with our decisions or opinions, but they will still love us and pray for and with us.

❑ Name a friend who was there when you were at the "bottom" and needed support. What did they do that was helpful to you?_____

_____

Remember, others may not have the privilege of receiving the special strength that comes to you through the prayers and friendship of your group. As you become aware of their needs, reach out to them.

## Scripture and Life

Praying women and praying men can make a difference for good in the world and in each other's lives. None of us should ever have to go through a serious problem without a group of praying friends.

The book of Esther illustrates what can happen when men and women pray. The story takes place about 486 B.C. in the Persian Empire. A number of the Jews have gone back to Israel to rebuild the country following years of captivity and enslavement. The King, Xerxes, also known as Ahasureus, becomes angry at his Queen Vashti during a royal party and removes her as Queen. Later he makes a decree that a queen will be chosen from among the young ladies of the empire.

Esther, a Jew and a niece to Mordecai, who works for the King, is selected Queen. One of the king's assistants, Haman, does not like Mordecai and wants him killed. In order to kill him, Haman convinces the king to pass a law that on a selected day, all Jews are to be destroyed. King Ahasureus does not know that his Queen is of Jewish origin and that he has sealed her death sentence.

When Mordecai hears of this tragic decision, he sends word to Esther about the decree of the King. Their conversation is recorded in Esther 4:10-17:

10) Then Esther spoke to Hathach, and gave him a command for Mordecai: 11) "All the king's servants and the people of the king's provinces know that any man or woman who goes into the inner court to the king, who has not been called, he has but one law; put all to death, except the one to whom the king holds out the golden scepter, that he may live. Yet I myself have not been called to go in to the king these thirty days." 13) So they told Mordecai Esther's words. 14) Then Mordecai told them to answer Esther: "Do not think in your heart that you will escape in the king's palace any more than all the other Jews. For if you remain completely silent at this time, relief and deliverance will arise for the Jews from another place, but you and your father's house will perish. Yet who knows whether you have come to the kingdom for such a time as this?" 15) Then Esther told them to return this answer to Mordecai: 16) "Go, gather all the Jews who are present in Shushan, and fast for me, neither eat nor drink for three days, night or day. My maids and I will fast likewise. And so I will go to the king, which is against the law; and if I perish, I perish!" 17) Then Mordecai went his way and did according to all the Esther commanded him.

❑ When faced with a serious problem in your life, what do you do?

☐ Tell no one but God.

☐ Get angry with God.

☐ Share it with a close friend.

☐ Tell my group and ask them to pray for me.

☐ Ignore it and hope it will go away.

☐ Other_____

❑ What was the solution Esther chose?_____

_____

_____

❑ How many people were involved in the solution?

_____

❑ The people were told to pray and to fast for Esther.
Have you ever fasted? (Yes or No) If so, for how
long?_____

_____

❑ What was the reason for your fast?_____

_____

_____

❑ Define the word *fast* as used in the context of
Esther's story._____

_____

_____

❑ What is the purpose of fasting?_____

_____

_____

One key reason for fasting is that it demonstrates
our readiness and desire to do God's will as we ask
Him to act on our behalf or for someone else in a
particular situation. (For further study, the following
passages are helpful. Matthew 6:16-18; 2 Chronicles
20:1-3; Daniel 10:1-3; Luke 10:17.)

❑ How can we know how long to fast—and when our fasting has accomplished its objective?_____

_____

_____

❑ If a person has medical problems (diabetes or hypoglycemia, for example) should they fast? Are there fasts other than a complete fast from all food and drink?_____

_____

_____

_____

❑ What kind of fasting is God speaking of in Isaiah 58:6?_____

_____

The results of prayer and fasting by Esther, Mordecai, and their friends were as follows:

♦ 5:1, 2—The King accepts Esther's visit.

♦ 6:1—The King can't sleep.

♦ 6:6—Mordecai is honored.

♦ 7:10—Haman is executed.

♦ 9:1-1—The Jews are saved.

❑ In 4:16, Esther asks the people to fast three days. What does this request reveal about her character and her faith in her people?_____

_____

_____

❑ What would happen if you asked for volunteers from your church to pray and fast with you?

_____

_____

❑ How would you be viewed?

   ❑ As someone who needs help.

   ❑ As someone seeking attention.

   ❑ As someone with a strange, outdated request.

   ❑ Other_____

The story of Esther and Mordecai projects our thoughts into the future—to a time when prophecy says God's people will face similar circumstances. The author of the book of Hebrews (11:32-38) spoke about persecution and miracles of faith:

> 32) And what more shall I say? For the time would fail me to tell of Gideon and Barak and Samson and Jephthah, also of David and Samuel and the prophets 33) who through faith subdued kingdoms, worked righteousness, obtained promises, stopped the mouths of lions, 34) quenched the violence of fire, escaped the edge of the sword, out of weakness were made strong, became valiant in battle, turned to flight the armies of the aliens. 35) Women received their dead raised to life again. And others were tortured, not accepting deliverance, that they might obtain a better resurrection. 36) Still others had trial of mocking and scourgings, yes, and of chains and imprisonment. 37) They were stoned, they were sawn in two, were tempted, were slain with the sword. They wandered about in sheepskins and goatskins, being destitute, afflicted, tormented—38) of whom the world was not worthy.

They wandered in deserts and mountains, in dens and caves of the earth.

Also, the history of the Dark Ages and the Reformation testify to the need for praying women and praying men (Revelation 12:1-6). Prior to the coming of Jesus, John also spoke of Satan's anger being unleashed against God's people.

"Then the dragon [Satan] was enraged with the woman [church], and he went to make war with the rest of her offspring, who keep the commandments of God and have the testimony of Jesus Christ" (Revelation 12:17).

It could be easy to be afraid, but listen to the promise of Jesus (Matthew 10:19, 20):

"But when they deliver you up, do not worry about how or what you should speak. For it will be given to you in that hour what you should speak; for it is not you who speak, but the Spirit of your Father who speaks in you."

Listen also to this beautiful promise of victory (Revelation 3:10-12):

"Because you have kept My command to persevere, I also will keep you from the hour of trial which shall come upon the whole world, to test those who dwell on the earth. Behold, I come quickly! Hold fast what you have, that no one may take your crown. He who overcomes, I will make him a pillar in the temple of My God, and he shall go out no more. And I will write on him the name of My God and the name of the city of My God, the New Jerusalem, which comes down out of heaven from My God. And I will write on him My new name."

How are one's thoughts kept on Jesus? Through a continual connection in prayer.

## Application to Life

❑ What are some Scriptures that give you faith and hope in Jesus?_____

_____

_____

_____

❑ What would you like God to do for you in your relationship with Him?

☐ Give you perseverance in life.

☐ Help you to fast and pray.

☐ Help you to have a faith that gives you strength like Esther and Mordecai.

☐ Make you a woman or man of prayer.

☐ Other

## Prayer Time

As your group prays together, pray through the list of responses to the question above and ask God to answer these requests in the lives of each group member.

# When Churches Pray

"As we meditate upon the perfections of the Saviour, we shall desire to be wholly transformed, and renewed in the image of His purity. There will be a hungering and thirsting of soul to become like Him whom we adore. The more our thoughts are upon Christ, the more we shall speak of Him to others, and represent Him to the world." —E.G. White.

## Group Life

Your group has been meeting for several weeks together. Friendships have developed. Spiritual bonding has occurred, and prayer has become a central focus of your life. This special relationship can continue in several ways.

First, after a brief break, group members whose schedules permit can meet together and continue their small-group experience.

Second, your personal prayer relationship with God can continue. The principles and concepts learned during the past few weeks can be continually applied on a daily basis.

Third, informal prayer partnerships can be formed for mutual encouragement. The men in your group can pair up with one another or even with other male acquaintances who have not been members of the group. The women can do the same. On a regular basis, by telephone, in person, or by letter, these partners can pray together, encourage each other, and share prayer needs.

❑ Share with one another what these studies on prayer and the group experience have meant to you. Also, what do you personally want to occur now in your own prayer life?_____

_____

_____

_____

_____

## Scripture and Life

It appears as if the war is over and enough time has passed that the enemy is forever defeated. Satan gloats as he looks upon the scene. The barren mountains loom up on each side of the vast desert floor. A lone vulture circles and moves on. A lizard, with flicking tongue, pauses momentarily beside one of the scattered, drying plants. The temperature at mid-day drives anything possessing life in search of shelter from the oppressive heat.

It is not an enjoyable sight. Skeletons of men, women, and children lie in heaps—scattered across the open plain. The sun, after many days, has bleached and cracked the bones. But God has in this unpleasant scene a lesson for His church.

Ezekiel 37:1-13 says:

1) The hand of the Lord came upon me and brought me out in the Spirit of the Lord, and set me down in the midst of the valley; and it was full of bones. 2) Then He caused me to pass by them all around, and behold, there were very many in the open valley; and indeed they were very dry. 3) And He said to me, "Son of man, can these bones live?" So I answered, "O Lord God, You know." 4) Again He said to me, "Prophesy to these bones, and say to them, 'O dry bones, hear the word of the Lord! 5) Thus says the Lord God to these bones: "Surely I will cause breath to enter into you, and you shall live. 6) I will put sinews on you and bring flesh upon you, cover you with skin and put breath in you; and you shall live. Then you shall know that I am the Lord."' 7) So I prophesied as I was commanded; and as I prophesied, there was a noise, and suddenly a rattling; and the bones came together, bone to bone. 8) Indeed as I looked, the sinews and the flesh came over them and the skin covered them over; but there was no breath in them. 9) Then He said to me, "Prophesy to the breath, prophesy, son of man, and say to the breath, 'Thus says the Lord God; Come from the four winds, O breath, and breathe on these slain, that they may live'." 10) So I prophesied as He commanded me, and breath came into them, and they lived, and stood upon their feet, an exceedingly great army. 11) Then He said to me, "Son of man, these bones are the whole house of Israel. They indeed say, 'Our bones are dry, our hope is lost, and we ourselves are cut off!' 12) Therefore prophesy and say to them, 'Thus says the Lord God: "Behold, O My people, I will open your graves and cause you to come up from your graves, and bring you into the land of Israel. 13) Then you shall know that I am the Lord, when I have opened your graves, O My people, and brought you up from your graves'."

The literal message to the prophet Ezekiel was simple. Even though the nation of Israel, God's people, were scattered and defeated, there was hope for revival and restoration.

The prophecy, however, has a dual application. It not only applied to literal Israel over 2,000 years ago, but it speaks also today to God's church.

## Verses 1, 2:

❑ Why do you believe God uses the imagery of human remains to talk about the condition of His people?_____

_____

_____

❑ Read 1 Corinthians 12:12-31. In what way does this passage help us in understanding Ezekiel's vision?

_____

_____

❑ What does the dryness of the bones represent?

_____

_____

## Verse 3:

❑ When God asked Ezekiel, "Can these bones live?" He . . .

☐ Wanted Ezekiel to say "Yes."

☐ Wanted to discover his level of faith.

☐ Wanted to challenge him to not be discouraged.

☐ Other_____

❑ What does God say is the first step in the revival of the bones?_____

_____

❑ What does this mean for us today?_____

_____

## Verses 5, 6:

❑ What is meant by the symbolism of the tendons, flesh, and skin being applied to the body?_____

_____

_____

## Verses 7, 8:

❑ In order for the skeletons to receive tendons, flesh, and skin, Ezekiel had to be involved. God, of course, didn't need Ezekiel to perform the miracle. Why do you think God used him?_____

_____

_____

❑ What is the significance of this for us today?_____

_____

_____

## Verses 9, 10:

The Hebrew language uses the word *ruach* for wind, breath, and spirit. How are these words related as used in verses 5, 9, and 14?_____

❑ Verses 7, 8, and 10 describe two steps in raising the dead. Why not do it all at once?_____

**Verses 11-14:**

❑ Apply verses 11-14 to the individual Christian life and to the Christian church today._____

In this vision, God summarizes our entire series of lessons about prayer. Prayer is a two-way communication between God and His people. When there is recognition of His sovereignty; dependence upon Him; commitment to His will, and an earnest desire to continually be connected to Him, we are empowered by the Holy Spirit. Prayer is the life link that revives the church and each of us as members. The bones were dry—no flesh was upon them, no life was in them—because the prayer relationship had malfunctioned or was nonfunctional.

When churches pray, there is power. When churches pray, there is revival. When churches pray, their members become like Jesus. When churches pray, people accept Jesus as Lord and Saviour. When churches pray, they are doing the work of God's kingdom.

## Application to Life

❑ As you consider the local church where you attend, what is its emphasis upon prayer? Is it discussed in church? Are there designated meetings for prayer? What is being done to assist individual members in their prayer journey?

_____

_____

_____

_____

❑ What suggestions do you have to help your local church in emphasizing prayer?_____

_____

_____

_____

❑ What steps can be taken to communicate your suggestions and feelings to the church leadership and to the congregation?_____

_____

_____

❑ Suggestions for a prayer emphasis in the local church:

   ♦ A series of sermons on prayer.

   ♦ Periodically have members share testimonies about their need for prayer and their experiences of answered prayer.

♦ Allow members to write prayer requests on slips of paper and collect them at church to be prayed about.

♦ Periodically ask members who have special prayer needs to come to the front of the church to receive special prayer, to raise a hand where they sit, to have a time of silent prayer in which the members pray for each other, or to make time occasionally for congregational conversational prayer.

♦ Form home groups and study this set of lessons during the week. If the setting and circumstances are appropriate, the pastor can preach on the same topic each Sabbath.

♦ Divide the names of the families in your church into 52 groups—a group for each week of the year. Each week at church, print the names of these families in your bulletin or on a special insert. Ask the congregation to pray specifically for the families at home that week—and to pray specifically by name for the families during the church services.

♦ Develop a Prayer Partner program in the local church. Have men form partnerships for prayer with other men—and women with other women. Include also the children and youth. Pray each day for your partner. Periodically discuss your prayer needs and joys with each other. Pray together in person or by phone.

♦ Organize prayer chains to pray for specific needs.

♦ Regularly hold meetings for prayer at your church or in homes.

♦ Study the topic of fasting and prayer, and apply the principles and concepts you learn to your individual life and to your church.

Your turn! What other suggestions can you think of?

_____

_____

_____

_____

_____

## Prayer Time

As you pray together as a group, pray . . .

♦ Specifically by name for each church congregation represented in your group.

♦ Specifically by name for the members of your group, that their prayer lives will grow and prosper.

♦ For a revival in the church worldwide.

♦ For the soon return of Jesus to this earth.

Remember: The object of Christ's supreme love is His church. No matter the condition of His people, God's love forgives them, changes them, and empowers them to be like Him in character and ministry.

# Acknowledgments and Sources

The thoughts, ideas, and concepts expressed in these lessons have evolved over time and in my personal experience. Ideas have been gleaned not only from books but from many other people. Joe Aldrich, for example, provided ideas and inspiration as I heard a presentation he made on the topic of prayer. Others whose contributions I wish to acknowledge include: Don and Ruthie Jacobsen, Larry Evans, Kevin Wilfley, Chad and Debi McComas, Janet Rowe, Jerry and Janet Page, Bob Dale, Monte Sahlin, Gordon Retzer, and Tom Baez—all of whom have worked closely with me in prayer conferences.

Other sources include:

Barclay, William, *Barclay's New Testament Commentary*, Philadelphia: The Westminster Press, 1975.

Bounds, E.M., *The Complete Works of E.M. Bounds on Prayer*, Grand Rapids, Mich.: Baker Book House, 1990.

_____, *The Possibilities of Prayer*, Chicago: Moody Press.

Chambers, Oswald, *Prayer: A Holy Occupation*, Grand Rapids, Mich.: Discovery House Publishers, 1992.

Coleman, Lyman, Ed., *Serendipity Bible for Groups*, Littleton, Colo.: Serendipity House, 1988.

Gordon, S.D., *Quiet Talks on Prayer*, Westwood, N.J.: Barbour and Company, Inc., 1984.

Hybels, Bill, *Too Busy Not to Pray*, Downers Grove, Ill.: InterVarsity Press, 1988.

*New King James Bible, The*, Nashville, Tenn.: Thomas Nelson Publishers, 1979, 1980, 1982.

Nichol, Francis D., Ed., *The Seventh-day Adventist Bible Commentary*, Washington, D.C.: Review and Herald Publishing Association, 1956.

Tirabassi, Becky, *Let Prayer Change Your Life*, Nashville, Tenn.: Thomas Nelson Publishers, 1992.

_____, *My Partner Prayer Notebook*, Nashville, Tenn.: Thomas Nelson Publishers, 1990.

_____, *Releasing God's Power*, Nashville, Tenn.: Thomas Nelson Publishers, 1990.

Venden, Morris, *The Answer Is Prayer*, Boise, Idaho: Pacific Press Publishing Association, 1988.

White, Ellen G., *The Acts of the Apostles*, Mountain View, Calif.: Pacific Press Publishing Association, 1911.

_____, *Christ's Object Lessons*, Washington, D.C.: Review and Herald Publishing Association, 1941.

_____, *The Desire of Ages*, Mountain View, Calif.: Pacific Press Publishing Association, 1898.

_____, *Prophets and Kings*, Mountain View, Calif.: Pacific Press Publishing Association, 1917.

_____, *Steps to Christ*, Washington, D.C.: Review and Herald Publishing Association, 1908.